BETTER!

THE NEW COVENANT IN HEBREWS

BY JOHN TERRELL

Published by:

HAYES PRESS

The Barn, Flaxlands

Royal Wootton Bassett

Swindon, SN4 8DY

United Kingdom

www.hayespress.org

Unless otherwise indicated, all Scripture quotations are from the Revised Version Bible, 1885 (Public Domain). Scriptures marked KJV are from the King James Version, 1611 (Public Domain).

Table of Contents

CHAPTER ONE: INTRODUCTION.....................................1

CHAPTER TWO: "THOU ART MY SON".......................6

CHAPTER THREE: THE AUTHOR OF OUR
SALVATION 12

CHAPTER FOUR: OUR CONFESSION AND REST ..18

CHAPTER FIVE: A LIVING WORD AND A GREAT
HIGH PRIEST 25

CHAPTER SIX: SPIRITUAL GROWTH AND SOLEMN
WARNING 32

CHAPTER SEVEN: A UNIQUE PRIESTHOOD 38

CHAPTER EIGHT: THE PERFECT HIGH PRIEST 45

CHAPTER NINE: COVENANTS OLD AND NEW 51

CHAPTER TEN: THE GOOD THING TO COME......56

CHAPTER ELEVEN: PERFECTED FOR EVER..............62

CHAPTER TWELVE: TO ENTER THE HOLY
PLACE 67

CHAPTER THIRTEEN: A FEARFUL THING 74

CHAPTER FOURTEEN: BY FAITH WE
UNDERSTAND 80

CHAPTER FIFTEEN: NOT ASHAMED TO BE CALLED THEIR GOD..84

CHAPTER SIXTEEN: LET US RUN WITH ENDURANCE...89

CHAPTER SEVENTEEN: EARTHLY DISCIPLINE – HEAVENLY VISION..94

CHAPTER EIGHTEEN: COMPLETE ... TO DO HIS WILL...100

CHAPTER ONE: INTRODUCTION

———

As we embark on a brief consideration of one of the most remarkable New Testament epistles, we shall examine the teaching of this book, unique among the New Testament letters to disciples in churches of God, and share thoughts also on the practical instruction it contains.

Careful instruction on doctrine in the Scriptures is always linked to a practical outcome in the lives and service of Christians, whether at the individual or the collective level. The teaching in this epistle is very specially directed towards the people of God. The way in which His people serves Him, particularly in priestly service, stands out in importance relative to their great High Priest, the Lord Jesus Christ.

A people is, of course, composed of individuals, and so there is much in Hebrews to challenge the heart of each disciple of Christ who aspires to share in the collective priestly service of the sanctuary "... the true tabernacle which the Lord pitched, not man" as described in chapter 8 verse 2. As we observe the comparisons and contrasts of the teaching of the Old Covenant on the one hand, and the New on the other, we shall ask who comprises the highly privileged company, the people of God, today; and relate the teaching of Hebrews about the house of God to other relevant scriptures in the New Testament.

First of all, let us think about this wonderful New Testament book as a whole; its principal purpose and its likely origins. It is wonderfully true that every scripture is inspired of God, as Paul assures Timothy in chapter 3 verse 16 (RV margin) of his second epistle to his younger fellow servant. And yet it is always valuable to note the human authorship of the books of the Bible; to observe, among other things, how the Lord the Spirit uses human gifts and experiences in presentation of divine truth. This is apparent as God expresses His thoughts through the minds of men prepared by Himself.

So, who wrote the epistle to the Hebrews? The truth is that we simply do not know for sure, and this being so, it is probably wiser not to spend too much time on speculation. The book was never seriously doubted as worthy of a place in the canon of New Testament scripture despite the uncertainty of the authorship. The spiritual quality of the language and doctrine strikes too high a note for that to have happened. Paul, Barnabas, Apollos, and others have been championed by different writers, and it has been suggested that we have Paul's thinking and Luke's writing! Certainly the lofty spiritual tone, and the authority and assurance of the instructions, might well incline us towards Paul as the author. But we simply have to leave the issue and move on to the interesting question of the likely date of Hebrews.

Again there is less certainty about this matter than there is about some letters to the New Testament churches. The direction of the teaching in keeping with the title of the book, is towards Jewish Christians, whether manly in Palestine or Rome, or both. Probably the best estimates as to dates is around 64-68 AD, about the time when the major Jewish war started, leading ultimately to the first century holocaust of AD 70/71, and the sacking and destruction of Jerusalem.

We have the impression from the writing that the Temple and its service still existed when the writer was at work on his treatise. Certainly, he makes it plain that the background of his writing is severe persecution of the disciples he is addressing. The passage at the end of chapter 10 draws attention to "a great conflict of sufferings". "For ye have need of patience, that, having done the will of God, ye may receive the promise". Part of that promise concerned the awaited return of their Lord. "For yet a very little while he that cometh shall come, and shall not tarry. But my righteous one shall live by faith".

The persecution referred to stemmed from adherence, on the one hand to the teaching of the Law of Moses, with its continuing temple sacrifice and worship; and on the other, to the vision of the divine service and worship of a New Covenant people of God. Not surprisingly, many Jews were trying to accommodate themselves to both, but the conflict and contrast involved was so apparent that a polarization inevitably took place. Rejection of the old inferior order prompted intense persecution of the disciples who had felt constrained to turn away from it to something infinitely better, centered on the Person of the Lord Jesus Christ. So it is not surprising that the word 'better' is a key word in this great epistle; and that it opens with a resounding declaration of excellences of the Saviour.

We shall return to say more of this in a later chapter, but for now let us note the basic structure of Hebrews. Commencing with a lofty appreciation of the Person of the eternal Son of God, the author proceeds to develop in some detail the theme of the superiority of the risen Christ, especially in His heavenly offices; superiority over all that was associated with the service and worship of the Old Covenant. This involves comparison and contrasts with the ancient prophets of Israel; with the exalted company of angels; with Moses the mediator of the Old Covenant; with Joshua, who succeeded Moses and led the people of Israel into the Promised Land; and with Aaron, the head of the priestly line which officiated in the tabernacle and Temple, standing between God and men, which is really the priestly function.

Linked to this is an exposition of the heavenly grandeur of "the true tabernacle, which the Lord pitched, not man", compared with the shadowy character of the early Tabernacle and Temple sanctuary which preceded it. Both the Person and the place associated with the worship of a New Covenant people become prominent as the writer develops his theme, and this carries as far as the middle of chapter 10. It is essential that no effort be spared in laying a secure foundation for the important appeal of chapter 10 verse 22: "Let us draw near with a true heart in fullness of faith, having our hearts sprinkled from an evil conscience, and our body washed with pure water." More on this in a future chapter.

Details of the priestly service of God's New Covenant people are not dealt with at any length in the book of Hebrews, and we can learn more about this from other New Testament scriptures. Rather, the author of Hebrews moves on into exhortations and warnings about the spiritual condition of disciples of Christ. This includes his monumental discourse in chapter 11 on faith, and the illustrious men and women of God who adorned that virtue with such distinction. Then, we have to "consider one another", to "lay aside every weight, and the sin which so easily doth beset us", to "run with patience", to "let brotherly love continue", and to "go forth unto him without the camp, bearing his reproach". These, and many other exhortations and encouragements close the epistle to the Hebrews, and leave us in awe at a biblical gem of immense value and solemn challenge.

CHAPTER TWO: "THOU ART MY SON"

———

We turn to the opening chapter of Hebrews and their sublime treatment of the person of Christ. The lofty themes of chapters 1 and 2, concern his glorious character, first as eternally superior in His deity to the highest of created beings – "Thy throne, O God, is for ever and ever"; and then, as the One who in the fullest sense really became man – "in all things to be made like unto his brethren". The assertion of the Lord's deity and true humanity in the opening two chapters of Hebrews, has often been compared to two majestic pillars through which we enter the spacious courtyard of doctrine which forms the rest of this marvelous letter.

So we begin with the first opening verse of chapter 1: "God having of old time spoken unto the fathers in the prophets by divers portions and in divers manner, hath at the end of these days spoken unto us in his Sin, whom he appointed heir of all things, through whom also he made the worlds; who being the effulgence of his glory, and the very image of his substance, and upholding all things by the word of his power, when he had made purification of sins, sat down on the right hand of the majesty on high."

These powerful words flow which such authority that it is almost impossible to break into them. Indeed, the entire opening chapter of Hebrews carries along the reader in a great sweep of praise of the divine Son of God, and leaves the angelic hosts, despite all their splendid dignity so far behind that the chapter closes with this reference of them, "Are they not all ministering spirits, sent forth to do service for the sake of them that shall inherit salvation?" This is no way detracts from the greatness of the hosts of heaven, but rather directs us to the vast superiority of the Son of God, who has "become by so much better than the angels, as has inherited a more excellent name than they".

A very telling occasion in Scripture which reveals the greatness of angelic beings in relation to men and women, is in Luke chapter 1. There Zacharias, the father of John the Baptist, responds to the angel's promise of a son in his old age. He asks, "Whereby shall I know of this? ... And the angel answering said unto him, I am Gabriel that stand in the presence of God" (vv.18,19). Gabriel was a being of awe-inspiring dignity, who had access to the very presence of Deity. When that same being appeared to Mary of Nazareth, he spoke in the most reverent terms of the Saviour to come. "He shall be great", he said, "and shall be called the Son of the Most High". Gabriel then responded to Mary's natural question, "How shall this be?" with the gentle rejoinder, "The Holy Spirit shall come upon thee, and the power of the Most High shall overshadow thee: wherefore also that which is to be born shall be called holy, the Son of God' (vv.34, 35). We can almost share the deep sense of awe Gabriel felt as he uttered those words about his majestic Lord.

Doubtless Gabriel felt overwhelmed at the far-reaching implication of his announcement of the birth of the eternal Son of God, "For", says Hebrews chapter 1 verses 5,6: "unto which of the angels said he at any time, Thou art my Son, this day have I begotten thee? And again, I will be to him a Father, and he shall be to me a Son? And when he again bringeth in the firstborn into the world he saith, and let all the angels of God worship him". These verses contain one of the most profound of all scriptural mysteries.

Abundant Bible evidence points to the eternal sonship of our Lord Jesus Christ. Consider one matter in particular, Paul's representation of Him in his letter to the Colossians. He writes of the Lord Jesus Christ as "the Son of his love", and says that, "in him were all things created, in the heavens and upon the earth, things visible and things invisible, whether thrones or dominions or principalities or powers; all thongs have been created through him and unto him; and he is before all things, and in him all things consist" (Col.1:16,17). We can readily see, therefore, that Moses' words in Psalm 90, "From everlasting to everlasting, thou art God", applying equally to the Lord Jesus as they do His Father.

What Hebrews chapter 1 verse 8 says is, "But of the Son he saith, Thy throne, O God, is for ever and ever". When Isaiah, by the Spirit, recorded his remarkable prophecy of the child to be born and the Son given, he added, "his name shall be called ... Everlasting Father", or as some versions have it, "Father of Eternity". As for angels, their place was one of worship. "And let all the angels of God worship him". When the apostle John was overcome in wonder at the things he heard in the

Revelation under the guidance of the angel, we read, "I fell down to worship before the feet of the angel which showed me these things. And he said unto me, See thou do it not ... worship God" (Rev.22:9).

It is very interesting and instructive to observe how the author of Hebrews employs the Old Testament scriptures here, and in particular the Psalms, to undergird his presentation of the Son of God. From Psalm 2 comes the declaration, "Thou art my Son; this day have I begotten thee". Probably from Psalm 89, and embracing 2 Samuel 7 and verse 12, we have the words, "I will be to him a Father, and he shall be to me a Son". Then we are taken to Psalm 104 for the quotation, "Who maketh his angel winds, and his ministers a flame of fire". This is a Psalm extolling the creative majesty of God. It includes the words, "O LORD, my God, thou art very great; thou art clothed with honor and majesty, who coverest thyself with light as with a garment, who stretchest out the heavens like a curtain".

Linking this with Paul's word in the Colossians epistle, we have no difficulty associating the Son of God with these lofty expressions of omnipotence. Then the beautiful Psalm 45 is quoted in the words, "the scepter of righteousness", and the divine anointing "with the oil of gladness above thy fellows".

Coming to Psalm 102, we have the citation: "Thou, Lord, in the beginning hast laid the foundation of the earth, and the heavens are the work of thy hands: they shall perish; but thou continuest: and they all shall wax old as doth a garment; and as a mantle shalt thou roll them up, as a garment, and they shall be changed: but thou art the same, and thy years shall not fail."

This is probably also a Psalm of David, and ascribes directly unto God, and to the Son of God also, the changelessness of Deity. Some of the scriptures quoted from the Psalms have a primary application in time to David; but a supreme application in doctrine to Christ, as demonstrated in Hebrews. Finally, in chapter 1 we have these words from Psalm 110, "Sit thou on my right hand, till I make thine enemies the footstool of thy feet." When we refer back to this Psalm itself we find these words prefaced by, "The LORD said unto my lord", the very words taken up by the Son incarnate when He challenged the unbelief of the Sadducees. "If David then calleth him Lord, how is he His son?" said Jesus (Matt.22:45).

Our thoughts soar upwards with the Psalmist and the writer of this epistle in adoration and worship of the eternal Son of God. Yet we do well to remember that the disciples receiving this epistle, who were greeted in the opening lines of the scroll with such uplifting truth about Christ, were under the shadow of severe religious persecution. This was from fellow Jews who tried to drag them back to what Paul called described to the Galatian Christians as "the weak and beggarly rudiments" of a form of worship which had been totally eclipsed by the brilliant revelation of the Son of God.

The strain of their daily harassment called for a vision to captivate their spirits; to lift their thought above; to enhance their appreciation of the place to which they had been brought in God's grace and of the Person of the Lord Jesus Christ. Every enemy of their souls must one day become His footstool.

Our burden of trial may be a different one today, but our need is the same, and our temptation to unbelief is just like theirs.

CHAPTER THREE: THE AUTHOR OF OUR SALVATION

———

"Therefore we ought to give the more earnest heed to the things that were heard, lest haply we drift away from them." This opening verse of chapter 2 of Hebrews injects a short warning passage between the theme of the deity of the Lord Jesus Christ, which dominates chapter 1, and the main subject of the second chapter, which is the true and perfect humanity of the Saviour, preparatory to His redemptive work. So why should these warning verses come in at this point? Verse 2 says, "For if the word spoken through angels proved stedfast, and every transgression and disobedience received a just recompense of reward; how shall we escape, if we neglect so great salvation?"

This salvation, says the writer, had been spoke through the Lord, and was confirmed by those who heard him. Moreover, God had enhanced their witness by miracles and gifts of the Holy Spirit as He willed. We must remember that those addressed in this letter were devout Jews who were struggling to come to terms with a whole new order of worship and service based on the ministry and sacrifice of Jesus. This short passage refers to something which had been very important to them hitherto, namely the important role of angels in connection with the giving of the law of Moses.

They are here being reminded, even before the second golden strand of truth about the humanity of the Lord is woven in, that the Law of Moses required obedience, and exacted a fitting penalty for disobedience. This principle still stands. When applied to this new revelation of God in Christ, it demanded their full attention and compliance. It is as though their spiritual teacher is saying to them, 'What I am now writing of is something established beyond all by the Lord, and commanding your total commitment. Give me your full attention while I expound to you God's great purpose in Christ'.

He then takes up again from the point where he had left off - angels and their exalted role. "For", we read, "not unto angels did He subject the world to come, whereof we speak". There follows a remarkable quotation from Psalm 8: "What is man, that thou art mindful of him: Or the son of man, that thou visitest him? Thou madest him a little lower than the angels; thou crownedst him with glory and honor, and didst set him over the works of thy hands: thou didst put all things in subjection under his feet."

Now there is no doubt that Psalm 8 has an application to mankind, to Adam and his progeny. Yet here is an application of primary importance to the incarnate Son of God. In many respects humankind is a lower order of animate creation compared with angels. Lower in authority and in the reflected glory that comes from the presence of God. We see this in connection with Gabriel. Into this order of humanity, with many of its physical limitation, and the ultimate experience of death, came the eternal son of God from heaven. From although He himself was without sin, yet as Paul says to Philippian Church, He became "obedient even unto death, yea, the death of the cross".

Let us take a few minutes to meditate on the deep significance of Psalm 8, as applied to Christ, as a man, for a while lower than the angels "because of the suffering of death"; yet also, "crowned with glory and honor". The divine purpose of grace was that "He should taste death for every man"; that the One "for whom are all things", that is God the Father Himself, might bring many sons to glory, and make the Author of their salvation, the Lord Jesus Christ, perfect, or complete, through suffering.

To do this, the scripture says, "it became him", or, "it was fitting". Why was it fitting for God, or why did it become Him, that His Son should suffer death? The answer is in verse 11, "for both he that sanctfieth and they that are sanctified are all of one: for which cause he is not ashamed to call them brethren". Having become truly a man, Jesus Christ, Son of God, must complete the work for which He had come by suffering death for His fellow-men.

This is the restoration of fallen man by the redemptive work of Christ on the cross, "bringing many sins unto glory". In chapter 10, verse 14 we read, "For by one suffering he hath perfected for ever them that are sanctified." Henceforth redeemed men and women are raised to a position that angels might well admire and revere. The redeemed are united eternally to Christ. He, and they, are now "all of one" as the scripture pus it. It is no coincidence that this is the point at which the Lord introduced that very precious designation of His own, namely "brethren".

Having "tasted death" and been made perfect through suffering, the Master chooses to refer to his disciples as "my brethren". "Go unto my brethren, and say to them ..." were the risen Lord's words to Mary in the garden of resurrection. Sons brought to glory – my brethren! What a precious, and indeed exciting, relationship is revealed here! Savor this, you downtrodden Jewish disciples; treasure and appreciate this standing you have in Christ. Has the Old Covenant anything comparable to offer? Is not this something vastly superior? God became man, 'for us men and for our salvation', as the old catechism eloquently expresses it.

Now verse 14 declares, "Since then the children are sharers in flesh and blood, he also himself in like manner partook of the same; that through death he might bring to naught him that had the power of death, that is, the devil." Space will not allow reference to each phrase, important as they all are to teaching of the passage. The point of verse 15 concerning the deliverance, or release, of those who though fear of death were all their lifetime subject to bondage, was of great significance to the Jewish Christians addressed. They certainly understood about the shadowy prospect which death brought to men and women of faith under the Old Covenant. Now, in Christ, to be "absent from the body" is to be "at home with the Lord" (2 Cor.5:8).

As the Lord Himself had promised, referring to the Church His Body, "the gates of Hades shall not prevail against it" – Hades, that uninviting prison house to which death brought Old Testament saints, is no part of the death experience of the Christian. Members of Christ make no acquaintance with such a place of confinement and waiting. Who would not exchange such a comforting hope for the shades of Old Testament prospects?

Finally, in Hebrews chapter 2, it is back to the angels for a farewell reference, where we are reminded that it was not with angels that but with "the seed of Abraham" that Christ was identified in His incarnation; it was not to angels that He was giving aid, as some translators put it, but to men and women in all the dire need of their fallen state. And what is more, the whole glorious work of salvation had more in view than deliverance from divine judgement. Another vista was to be opened up for, when "in all things" he had "to be made like unto His brethren", it was in order: "that he might be a merciful and faithful high priest in things pertaining to God, to make propitiation for the sins of the people. For in that he himself hath suffered being tempted, he is able to succour them that are being tempted."

We can imagine those who received this letter reading, re-reading and pondering these words. As Jews they knew about high priests, and what they had seen of them in their own lifetime would hardly inspire confidence. They also knew a lot about temptation, temptation to go back, temptation to renounce their new faith. These strong, instructive, encouraging words about the Lord Jesus would surely stiffen their resolve, and help them grasp the truth later expressed in Hebrews 12:2, "looking unto Jesus, the author and perfecter of our faith."

CHAPTER FOUR: OUR CONFESSION AND REST

———

We come now to chapter 3, and part of chapter 4, in our consideration of the epistle to the Hebrews. There are many "therefore's" and "wherefore's" in this epistle and chapter 3 opens with one of these. This is entirely appropriate since the opening two chapters have presented Christ so perfectly in His full deity and true humanity. Such a portrayal of the eternal Son of God in His redemptive work of bringing many sons unto glory must contain a challenge. And here it is: "consider the Apostle and High Priest of our confession, even Jesus."

The author of Hebrews was about to launch into an extended passage of teaching about the high priestly work of the risen Christ in relation to the people of God in the house of God. But first, the disciples are reminded of the rounded and complete ministry of Christ as the Apostle, the sent One who has now gone into heaven to accomplish a priestly service for God's people. Moreover, the disciples are addressed as "holy brethren, partakers of a heavenly calling". The sons brought to glory, and declared by the Lord Jesus to be "my brethren", are now reminded that holiness must characterize them; their calling is heavenly. And so we move on to a studied comparison between the service of the great Moses who related to God's house of Old Covenant times and the role of Christ in God's spiritual house today.

Christ Jesus, we read in verses 2-6 of chapter 3: "was faithful to him that appointed him, as also was Moses in all his ('God's' - RV margin) house. For he hath been counted worthy of more glory than Moses, by so much as he that built the house hath more honor than the house. For every house is built by some one; but he that built all things is God. And Moses indeed was faithful in all his house as a servant, for a testimony of these things which were afterward to be spoken; but Christ as a son, over his house; whose house are we, if we hold fast our boldness and the glorifying of our hope firm unto the end."

In considering chapter 1 we saw that this letter, which was addressed to converted devout Jews, set out to demonstrate the complete superiority of Christ, first of all compared to angels, then to some of the major heroes of the Jewish people. Not surprisingly, Moses comes first, because the central theme is a comparison and contrast between the Old Covenant, of which he was the mediator, and the New Covenant, established and presented by Christ. Moses had indeed been a faithful servant in God's house in the wilderness. He had dutifully ensured that everything was made according to the pattern he had been shown in Mount Sinai. And he had carefully administered everything associated with the service of the Tabernacle, leaving the priestly service to his brother Aaron and his sons, as God had directed. Moses knew his place and filled it with distinction, but it was the place of a servant in God's house. Christ's place today is that of Son over God's house.

We read in John's Gospel of the day the Lord Jesus debated true faith and discipleship with a group of unbelieving Jews, people well versed in the law and writings of Moses, as were the recipients of the Hebrews epistle. Here are some of Christ's words: "the bondservant" (or slave) He said, "abideth not in the house for ever: the son abideth for ever. If therefore the Son shall make you free, ye shall be free indeed" (John 8:35,36). Although the context was different from that in Hebrews chapter 3, there is a clear principle contained in the Lord's words, and one which Jews would readily appreciate. Servants might be distinguished by skills and diligence, but the sons of the household were of a different order, and so point to the superiority of the new order over the old.

But we need to pause here and note the words of verse 6, "whose house are we, if we hold fast our boldness and glorifying of our hope firm unto the end". We shall find various warning passages in Hebrews – indeed we met the first in chapter 2 about the danger of spiritual drift – and in all these passages we need to remember clearly that those addressed had known the regenerating power of the Holy Spirit. They were men and women who belonged to Christ through faith, and this underlying assumption is clear in the writer's mind at all points in this letter. Even in the most trenchant warning passage, as we shall see when we come to, chapter 10, we find that this issue is the Lord's judging of His people, not eternally condemning unbelieving persons who have rejected Christ when presented to them; not people who have never known "the washing of generation and renewing of the Holy Spirit" as Paul describes the experience of conversion when writing to Titus (Titus 3:5). "Holding fast" is about service, not salvation from sin's penalty.

It is important to establish this matter clearly in studying the epistle to the Hebrews, and here in chapter 3 a conditional element emerges: "if we hold fast ...". This applies as we see to the house of God, and the disciples addressed here along with those in other New Testament churches of God, constituted that "house of God". We shall have occasion to return to this point, but meantime we go on to note the quotation from Psalm 95 which immediately follows: "Today if ye shall hear his voice, harden not your hearts, as in the provocation, like as in the day of the temptation in the wilderness" – and so on, in reference to the failure of Israel in their pilgrimage to the land of promise. Because of this, we read, "As I sware in my wrath, they shall not enter into my rest". Then follows the stern application of this to the Hebrew Christians who were under strong pressure to fail in a similar way in their own day:

"Take heed, brethren, lest haply there shall be in any one of you an evil heart of unbelief, in falling away from the living God: but exhort one another day by day, so long as it is called Today; lest any one of you be hardened by hardened by the deceitfulness of sin; for we are become partakers of Christ, if we hold fast the beginning of our confidence firm unto the end."

Mutual encouragement among Christians is a much-neglected spiritual exercise, but one we do well to practice carefully, Sin's deceptions are insidious and make for hard and disobedient hearts towards the Lord and His gracious high priestly work. Further reminder is added about the disobedience and displeasing behavior of the Israelites who came out of Egypt, who provoked the Lord God to anger, and who died in the wilderness as a result. With all the Promised Land before them, "we see that they were not able to enter in because of unbelief". Such then is the doleful summary of the experience of Israel in the past.

Let us note with care and interest the use of the expression "my rest", for in the first part of chapter 4 this thought is pursued and developed. "Let us fear therefore, lest haply a promise being left of entering into his rest, any one of you should seem to have come short of it." Then, in verse 3 of chapter 4, in words, "for we which have believed do enter into that rest." The thought is linked to the resting by God on the seventh day of creation, and another prospect of entering into rest is expounded. This is based on the quotation from Psalm 95, words written long after the wilderness failure of Israel: "For if Joshua had given them rest, he would not have spoken afterward of another day. There remaineth therefore a Sabbath rest for the people of God ... Let us therefore give diligence to enter into that rest that no man fall after the same example of disobedience."

What is the "rest" discussed here? Clearly it is something in God's purpose for his present day people and, as we have seen, it is closely linked with the service of God's house and our obligation of obedience. God's word through Moses and Aaron to Pharaoh in Egypt was, "Let my people go, that they may serve me" (Ex.7:16). The ultimate scene of that service was to be in land of God's promise to the patriarchs. So the thought of "rest", of "service", and of God's "house" come together and present us with a picture of a settled place of service for disciples of Christ today in the house of God. This carries our thoughts back to the Lord's words in Matthew chapter 11, "come unto me, all ye that labor and are heavy laden, and I will give you rest. Take my yoke upon you, and learn of me; for I am meek and lowly in heart: and ye shall find rest unto your souls. For my yoke is easy, and my burden is light." Two rests, a rest to be *given* by Christ to weary sinner, and a rest to be *found* as we bear His yoke in obedient service.

We shall come on to speak further of the service of God's house in relation to the "true sanctuary" as described in chapter 8, and all in the sublime context of the high priestly service of Christ; as well as commenting on some other scriptures which extend our understanding of the service of God's house today. The beleaguered Hebrew Christians receiving this letter were being presented with the surpassing excellence of their spiritual lot in Christ, compared with what was old and vanishing. As heirs with them of this grand inheritance, we too can respond with joy and obedience to this unfolding of God's purpose of grace.

———————

The veil is rent! Lo, Jesus sits

Upon a throne of grace;

The incense which his name emits

Fills all that glorious place.

His precious blood is sprinkled there

Before and on the throne

And His own wounds in heaven declare

His work on earth is done.

"Tis finished," on the cross he said

In agonies and blood,

"Tis finished," now he lives to plead

Before the face of God.

"Tis finished," here our souls can rest,

His work can never fail;

By Him, our Sacrifice and Priest,

We enter through the veil.

Within the Holiest of all,

Cleansed by His precious blood,

Before Thy throne, Thy people fall,

And worship Thee, O God.

Boldly our heart and voice we praise,

His name, His blood, our plea,

Assured our sacrifice of praise,

Ascends by Him to Thee.

CHAPTER FIVE: A LIVING WORD AND A GREAT HIGH PRIEST

———

In the last chapter, we reached chapter 4 of the epistle where the writer appeals to the Jewish believers who were beset by the temptation to return to an inferior faith. Their ancestors failed through disobedience to enter God's rest for them in the land of promise. But another rest was in view in the service of God's spiritual house today.

So, verse 11 of chapter 4 says, "Let us therefore be diligent to enter that rest, lest anyone fall after the same example of disobedience." It is as though the very thought of disobedience to the commands of God prompts the writer here to make a solemn declaration about the nature of the word of the Lord; and to do this before he proceeds with the development of his thoughts about Jesus, the Son of God, as great High Priest. The words used have come to rank as one of the most profound and challenging of all statements about the Word of God: "For the word of God is living and powerful, and sharper than any two-edged sword, piercing even to the division of soul and spirit, and of joints and marrow, and is a discerner of the thoughts and intents of the heart. And there is no creature hidden from His sight, but all things are naked and open to the eyes of Him to whom we must give account" (vv.12,13).

These are powerful words, words which do not invite much in the way of commentary, but rather command prompt assent and worship. God's insight into our hearts is unerring and penetrating; no concealment of motive behind action; no shielding of hypocrisy where the eye of God sees. The agent of this perfect insight into the deepest recesses of our minds and hearts is the Word of God. Having laid that challenging consideration on the hearts of the disciples, the epistle goes on to some of the most precious words ever written about Jesus, the Son of God, in relation to His people. He is "a great High Priest who has passed through the heavens", we read, and we are encouraged to "hold fast our confession". He "passed through the heavens" - an expression we cannot comprehend fully, but which conveys a profound sense of the highly exalted place Christ now occupies.

Having passed through the heavens, He is seen to show a most gracious understanding of our human condition, and the comforting invitation is given to "draw near": "For we do not have a High Priest who cannot sympathize with our weaknesses, but was in all points tempted as we are, yet without sin. Let us therefore come boldly to the throne of grace, that we may obtain mercy and find grace to help in time of need (vv.15,16)." Much remains to be said about the glories and excellencies of the divine High Priest. Many instructive things have still to be offered in the epistle about the excellence of His unique ministry; about the absolute holiness of the heavenly place in which that ministry is fulfilled; and about the reality and substance, in contrast to the shadows which preceded it in Israel's past

But for now, enjoy, you hard-pressed Hebrew Christians, this unfolding of His lovely character. He can "sympathize with our weaknesses" says the New King James Version. He can "be touched with the feeling of our infirmities", as the Revised Version has it. It would need a whole series of eloquent words and phrases to do justice to such a thought. For He "was in all points tempted as we are, yet without sin". Our minds fail to comprehend all that is involved in the subject of the temptations of Christ. But our spirits find rest and peace in the good words of Scripture, and in the assurance of the sinlessness of the One who was in all things made like His brethren that He might indeed be such a merciful and faithful High Priest as here described.

So it is with the boldness of complete confidence that we can approach the throne of grace – a place combining majestic power, a throne; and kindly provision, grace. Here we find the mercy and grace that meet the demands of every time of need. It is not difficult to imagine a prayerful pause in the original reading of this letter, as the disciples reflected on these words. There was nothing to compare with this in their early spiritual experience in Judaism. No priest of Israel measured up to this. Here is access for the Lord's New Testament people to the very presence of Deity, mediated by the Son of God Himself, who by the way of Calvary, "has become higher than the heavens" (7:26).

Of course, those receiving the epistle were no strangers to the Old Testament revelation of the loving character of God, even if their previous service had not offered such amazing intimacy. In Psalm 103 David had declared, "As a father pities his children, so the LORD pities those who fear Him. For He knows our frame, He remembers that we are dust' (vv.13,14). And again, "the mercy of the LORD is from everlasting to everlasting on those who fear Him" (v.17). Yes, God knows our "frame". The Creator has nothing to learn about us, though men and women will go on learning till the end of time. But the High Priest who occupies the throne of grace, who was made in all things like His brethren, had entered right into the human condition. He had been made perfect, or complete, through suffering. Such a revelation brings sweet peace to troubled and fearful spirits.

Having turned aside, no doubt in quiet thanksgiving and worship, our Jewish brothers and sisters of those days would be well prepared to proceed to the next words of the epistle. These elaborate further upon the Father's preparation of His Son for the wonderful offices He now bears. Coming now to chapter 5, we are reminded that: "every high priest taken from among men is appointed for men in things pertaining to God, that he may offer both gifts and sacrifices for sins. He can have compassion on those who are ignorant and going astray, since he himself is also beset by weakness" (vv.1,2).

All of this was quite familiar to the disciples reading it. They would readily give their assent, and also to the further point that such priests required to sacrifice for the people *and* for themselves. Furthermore, the office was by divine, not human, calling, as Aaron knew. Again, they understood this very well. Now for the related teaching about Christ. "So also Christ did not glorify Himself to become High Priest" (v.5). The Father who had declared Him Son by eternal begetting, appointed Him "a priest for ever according to the order of Melchizedek".

The revelation which follows about the Lord Jesus in "the days of His flesh", stirs the spirit to wonder and worship. He is seen offering prayers and supplications with vehement cries and tears to Him who was able to save Him out of death, and being heard because of His godly fear. Is this truly the sinless Son of the Father who, though He was a Son, learned obedience by the things He suffered? Indeed, it is. He learned the *price*, not the *practice* of obedience. Disobedience was alien to His holy nature. "And having been perfected, (that is, made complete in experience and suffering) He became the author of eternal salvation to all who obey Him, called by God as High Priest according to the order of Melchizedek" (vv.9,10). The preciousness and solemnity of this teaching about the suffering of Christ should not be lost on us, as we trust it was not lost on those who first received it.

Again, we find ourselves laying the words alongside Paul's to the Philippians, "He humbled Himself and became obedient to the point of death, even the death of the Cross Therefore God also has highly exalted Him and given Him the name which is above every name" (2:8,9). Among the noble titles attributed to the risen Christ is this; "called by God as High Priest according to the order of Melchizedek, of whom we have much to say, and hard to explain, since you have become dull of hearing". In due course, we shall come to some of the things to be said about Melchizedek as the amazing role-model for our Lord's eternal priesthood.

———————

Done is the work that saves,

Once and for ever done!

Finished the righteousness

That clothes th' unrighteous one!

The love that blesses us below

Is flowing freely to us now.

The sacrifice is o'er,

The veil is rent in twain,

The mercy seat is red,

With blood of Victim slain.

Why stand we, then, without in fear?

The blood of Christ invites us near.

The gate is open wide,

The new and living way

Is clear and free and bright,

With love and peace and day,

Into the Holies now we come

Our present and eternal home.

Enthroned in majesty

The Great Priest sits within.

The precious blood once shed

Has made and keeps us clean.

With boldness let us now draw near,

That blood has banished every fear.

To Him who has been slain,

Be glory, praise and power;

He died, and lives again.,

He lives for evermore.

He loves us, cleansed us by His blood,

Made us a kingdom, priests to God.

CHAPTER SIX: SPIRITUAL GROWTH AND SOLEMN WARNING

———

At the end of chapter 5 of the epistle to the Hebrews the writer introduces a note of seeming rebuke for what he called dullness of hearing. Having spent precious words on a moving account of the humility and suffering of the Lord Jesus Christ on His way to His present seat at God's right hand, our writer is ready to move on to matters which call for mature spiritual understanding.

We have been introduced to the name Melchizedek and are promised things about him in relation to Christ which are "hard to explain". But these Jewish disciples did not yet inspire confidence in the writer of the epistle, because he perceived them as spiritually immature. "For though by this time you ought to be teachers", he said, "you need someone to teach you against first principles of the oracles of God" (v.12).

This might all sound to us a little harsh as addressed to Christians who were under some pressure and perhaps naturally rather preoccupied with their difficulties. Yet they were obviously well known to their correspondent who clearly felt the need to jolt them a little with his rather severe words. Your need is for milk, he declares, when it should be for solid food; you are still unskilled in the word of righteousness. Those of full age, or true maturity, have their senses exercised to discern both good and evil. In a very contrasting style, the apostle Peter, writing to the pilgrims of the Jewish Dispersion in a scattering of provinces, addresses them as "newborn babes" and encourages them, as such, to "desire the pure milk of the word, that you may grow thereby" (1 Pet.2:2). There is a time when perceptive spiritual teachers will nurse along gently believers in the churches of God; and another time when it is right to introduce a sharper note to deal with failure to grow after adequate opportunity and teaching.

So it seems to have been with the Hebrews to whom this epistle was written. But the note of admonition is not harped on. For next in chapter 6, verse 1 we have the words, "therefore, leaving the discussion of the elementary principles of Christ, let us go on to perfection". A foundation of the doctrine had been carefully laid down for them in such matters as repentance and faith, on baptisms, laying on of hands, resurrection, judgment. It was now time, God permitting for advancement to very important teaching on priestly service, based on the priestly office of Christ, and the Holy Spirit's instruction on the heavenly, spiritual sanctuary.

Yet although the next step was to promote deeper spiritual understanding of God's purposes for his people. it was necessary first of all to press home the grave danger of spiritual regression; not just the risk of stunted growth already referred to, but the hazard of a more catastrophic fall. And so we come in verses 4 to 8 of chapter 6 to one of the solemn warning passages of Hebrews. We must be in no doubt that those seen here at great spiritual risk are true believers, born again persons who have become the target of Satan's attack.

"For", we read: "it is impossible for those who were once enlightened, and have tasted the heavenly gift, and have become partakers of the Holy Spirit, and have tasted the good word of God and the powers of the age to come, if they fall away, to renew them again to repentance, since they crucify again for themselves the Son of God and put Him to an open shame." Clearly they were born again people. What, then, might they fall away from? An illustration from nature follows which provides an explanation. Sometimes, when rain falls on the earth, instead of yielding useful, nourishing plants, reflecting God's blessing, it brings forth thorns and briars, "near", we read, "to being cursed, whose end is to be burned". The words, "whose end is to be burned" must have brought the readers of this letter up sharply. As with ourselves, it must have led them to ponder the meaning of such strong statements. We are dealing here with the horrifying possibility of believers openly and aggressively repudiating their faith and profession, so that they exclude themselves from the possibility of repentance.

There is no prospect for them but inevitable divine judgement. Is this the judgement of hell, as some might be inclined to assume because of the analogy of the burning of the worthless thorns and briars? No! It is the burning of what the land produces, not of the land itself. So the illustration helps us understand that what is produced in a Christian's life is what may be burned, his works, and not the believer himself. So our eternal security is not involved here. That is safe in the Lord's keeping. Do we then have guidance else-where in the New Testament which takes account of the fearful thought of destruction by burning? We have. In 1 Corinthians chapter 3 we have a description of building for God in a believer's life, building on the foundation of Jesus Christ a life of service, the value of which may vary widely. Mentioned are gold, silver, precious stones, wood, hay, stubble. The descent in order of value becomes ever more steep until we arrive at stubble in all its worthlessness. Stubble is for burning. The analogy is with the life of a person whose service is described thus, "If anyone's work is burned, he will suffer loss; but he himself will be saved, yet so as through fire" (v.15).

This interpretation of these disturbing verses of warning in Hebrews chapter 6 is reinforced by the words which immediately follow in verse 9. "But, beloved, we are confident of better things concerning you, yes, things that accompany salvation, though we speak in this manner." Those whose Christian lives deteriorate into disorder, still have eternal salvation; but there is nothing accompanying salvation to glorify God and honor the Saviour; quite the reverse. These dear saints had to their great credit their "work and labour of love which you have shown towards His name". They had ministered in practical ways to the saints and are now encouraged to continue in this and to imitate their revered Jewish patriarchs who, through patient faith, had realized promises long ago given by God.

Not surprisingly, reference is now made to Abraham. In verse 13 we read, "For when God made a promise to Abraham, because he could swear by no one greater, He swore by Himself". He promised to bless and multiply Abraham and, after patient endurance, the promise was realized. An oath, even among men, is a solemn thing in God's sight, even if not always so in their own. So God, we are told, affirmed His promise with an oath to confirm the immutability of His counsel. Two unchangeable things, God's word of promise and the oath of a God who cannot lie, provide strong consolation for us who, as verse 18 says, "have fled for refuge to lay hold of the hope set before us. This hope we have as an anchor of the soul, both sure and steadfast, and which enters the Presence behind the veil, where the forerunner has entered for us, even Jesus, having become High Priest for ever according to the order of Melchizedek."

The author of Hebrews has sobered up his readers to the possibility of grievous failure, but immediately gone on to express confidence in them, based on their record of service. He now points to the unshakeable hope founded on the complete faithfulness of God, and deftly returns the subject to Christ, here described as our forerunner. The sure and steadfast hope spoken of here as an anchor of the soul, refers to our confidence on the promise of entering by faith within the veil, through our heavenly High Priest.

Holy, holy, holy, we now come before Thee

Gathered in that holy name so very dear to Thee.

O Lord God, we own Thee, humbly we adore Thee,

For Thy grace and power and truth and love we see.

Thou Thy Son hast given, see His body riven,

Pierced with cruel thorn and spear upon Gologatha's tree.

For our sins He suffered, and His body offered,

And His blood outpoured a sacrifice to Thee.

Now through Jesus' merit, gathered by the Spirit,

Here within the holy place, through Him we boldly come;

Hearts and voices blending, praise to Thee ascending.

Through our great High Priest we worship Thee alone.

Holy, holy, holy, humbly we adore Thee,

Honour, blessing, power and might we would ascribe to Thee;

Courts of heaven ringing with the praise we're bringing,

For the One who lives our living Lord to be.

CHAPTER SEVEN: A UNIQUE PRIESTHOOD

━━━

We now come to chapter 7 of the Hebrews epistle where the author, after several passing mentions finally takes up his discussion of the Melchizedek priesthood of Christ. In three short verses the salient points about Melchizedek's person and life are summarized:

"For this Melchizedek, king of Salem, priest of the Most High God who met Abraham returning from the slaughter of the Kings, and blessed him, to whom also Abraham gave a tenth part of all, first being translated 'king of righteousness', and then also 'king of Salem', meaning 'king of peace', without father, without mother, without genealogy, having neither beginning of days nor end of life, but made like the Son of God, remains a priest continually. Now consider how great this man was, to whom even the patriarch Abraham gave a tenth of his spoils."

Considering how important this man and his ministry is to this person and the priesthood of Christ, we are tempted to borrow a style of words used in another context altogether by Sir Winston Churchill and say. "Never were so few words spoken, in short a space, about so important a person." Melchizedek lived at the time of Abraham, that is about 1,900 years before Christ was born. He was king of a small nation, or tribe, and in all probability reigned in the city destined to be Jerusalem of lasting fame. He was also a priest, the first mention in the Bible of such an office, designated "priest of the Most High God". For about a thousand years nothing more was said of him in the Old Testament Scriptures; that is until David came on the scene and started writing divinely inspired poetry. This included Psalm 110 which is where the name Melchizedek re-appears.

In Genesis chapter 14 we seem to have a fascinating glimpse of what was a devout system of worship of the true God, before He chose Abraham to spearhead His future plans for a holy nation, Israel. We assume Melchizedek belonged to one of the Semitic tribes, or nations, to whom God had given some revelation of Himself. And God obviously recognized the priesthood Melchizedek served in. How widespread was this worship of God then? How many places has priests? All tantalizing, unanswered questions. And David in Psalm 110 does not fill us in any further on personal details about Melchizedek. The Holy Spirit's purpose through David was to introduce us to the spiritual significance of this remarkable historical figure.

"The LORD said unto my Lord, 'Sit at my right hand till I make Your enemies Your footstool'". So the psalm opens, and it is these words that the Lord took up with the Pharisees to show that "my Lord" referred to Himself. This established beyond all doubt that the person being addressed in prophecy is Psalm 110 is the coming One, the Lord Jesus Christ. One of the promises contained from Him in the Psalm, based on a divine oath, is, "You are a priest for ever, according to the order of Melchizedek".

After that we have nothing more in scripture about Melchizedek till we come to Hebrews and this succinct summary of Melchizedek's life and service. It includes a reminder of the conflict in which Abraham became involved on behalf of Lot. Returning from the rout of the ten kings, Abraham was met by Melchizedek who provided comforting refreshment, and assurance of divine blessing before the tempting blandishments of the king of Sodom could be offered. That action by Melchizedek foreshadowed most beautifully the future heavenly ministry of Christ, of which we have already though in looking at chapter 2, verse 18, "He is able to aid (succor, give comfort to) those who are tempted". Moreover, we read here in chapter 7, verse 2, "to whom also Abraham gave a tenth part of all". So Melchizedek became the person who gave comfort and support; who conferred divine blessing; and who received an offering. That precisely prefigures the high priestly work of Christ.

Now as well as being closely linked together in the matter of their priestly office, Melchizedek and Christ are identified with one another in other respects. We are told that Melchizedek was "king of righteousness" and "king of peace". These were translation of Melchizedek's name and title and they certainly reflected the character of his office. But their application in fullest reality belonged to Christ, the righteous Prince of peace.

Only in passing do we now note the total separation in God's law for Israel of the offices of priest and king. Even the king was excluded as a "stranger" as far as priestly service was concerned

(Num.3:10). When this was flouted, as by Uzziah, severe judgment resulted (2 Chr.26:16-23). After Melchizedek, no one, till the Lord Himself, received both offices.

That Melchizedek should be described as "without father, without mother, without genealogy, having neither beginning of days nor end of life, but made like the Son of God", tends to strike a note of mystery in our minds. We conclude, not that Melchizedek was any kind of human freak without natural antecedents, but that Scripture is dramatically presenting us with a snapshot of a remarkable historical character, directing our view exclusively to the man and the office which appears to have been unique to him.

The climax of the description is that he was "made like the Son of God". The Lord Jesus Christ, Son of God, has no beginning, no end. He *is* the beginning and the end as He declared to John on Patmos, 'I am the Alpha and the omega, the First and the Last' (Rev.1:11). This is also bound up in the final statement of verse 3 about Melchizedek who, we read, "remains a priest continually". It is as though the glimpse we have been given of Melchizedek in his unique and wonderful office is "frozen" on the page of Scripture; and all to impress upon us the unending character of the priestly office of the One for whom Melchizedek was that ancient role-model.

Now we might think that all of this is sufficient to impress upon us the greatness of Melchizedek as he foreshadowed our great heavenly High Priest. But verse 4 of Chapter 7, which we are considering, begins with the words, "Now consider how great this man was". We have more yet to learn of his importance before we go on to consider the instructive contrast between the priesthood of Aaron and that of Melchizedek. And the further instruction from Melchizedek is based on the law of tithing in the nation of Israel. In truth this law for God's people was enacted long after Abraham offered Melchizedek a tenth of all. This first mention of the tithe in Scripture in Genesis chapter 14, provides a preview of God's purpose on this matter for Israel.

As our text in Hebrews chapter 7 shows, we are looking from the perspective of the first century AD with full knowledge of how tithing had developed historically. It was those belonging to the family of Abraham's descendant Levi who received and administered tithing. Yet Levi was as verse 10 states, "still in the loins of his father Abraham" when the latter was met by Melchizedek, received the tithe from Abraham who, since he was the forefather of the priestly tribe, might reasonably have expected to receive, rather than give. Abraham was rewarded with Melchizedek's blessing and, verse 7 says, "beyond all contradiction the lesser is blessed by the better. Here mortal men receive tithes, but there he receives them, of whom it is witnessed that he lives." This says nothing about death, nothing about the mortality to which the Levites were subject.

All of this may sound to us a little complex, and not very easy to follow in its detail, but the main message is clear. Melchizedek was pointing forward to something, and someone who would occupy a priestly office vastly superior to that of the priests of Israel; with characteristics which were both better in every respect and, even more importantly, were eternal. This is the heavenly priesthood of Christ on behalf of the people of God.

The remainder of chapter 7, and the opening verses of chapter 8, complete the teaching about the priestly office of Christ and we shall consider this further in the next chapter. Thereafter, the heavenly place of the priestly service of God's people becomes prominent, and we will reflect later in some depth on the entrance there of our glorious forerunner, by His own blood; and all the excellencies of associated New Covenant truth.

———————

Th'atoning work is done,

The Victim's blood is shed.

And Jesus now is gone

His people's cause to plead.

He lives in heaven, their great High Priest

And bears their names upon His breast.

He sprinkled with His blood

The mercy-seat above,

For Justice had withstood

The purposes of Love.

But Justice now withstands no more

And Mercy yields her boundless store.

No temple made with hands

His place of service is;

In heaven itself He stands,

A heavenly priesthood His;

In Him the shadows of the law

Are all fulfilled and now withdraw.

And though awhile He may be

Hid from the eyes of men,

His people look to see

Their great High Priest again.

In brightest glory He will come

And take his waiting people home.

CHAPTER EIGHT: THE PERFECT HIGH PRIEST

The opening verse of the passage of Hebrews we are now considering is verse 11 of chapter 7, where the key word is "perfection". "Therefore, if perfection were through the Levitical priesthood (for under it the people received the law), what further need was there that another priest should arise according to the order of Melchizedek, and not be called according to the order of Levi?"

What follows is an extended explanation of the incompleteness, or imperfection, of the priesthood based on the family of Aaron and the Levites; and a discussion of the contrast with Christ's priesthood in heaven. The perfection, or completeness, of the Lord's priestly office depended on various factors and required, as verse 12 points out, a change of the law, that is the law of priestly succession hitherto centred on the tribe of Levi. "For", says verse 14, "it is evident that our Lord arose from Judah of which tribe Moses spoke nothing concerning priesthood."

But it was not just the law of tribal succession that required revision. Something much more fundamental was involved. Verse 15 says, "And it is yet far more evident, if in the likeness of Melchizedek, there arises another priest who has come, not according to the law of a fleshly commandment, but according to the power of an endless life. For he testifies: 'You are a priest forever according to the order of Melchizedek.' For on the one hand there is an annulling of the former commandment because of its weakness and unprofitableness, for the law made nothing perfect; on the other hand, there is the bringing in of a better hope, through which we draw near to God."

So now we see the omission of any mention of "beginning of days or end of life" for Melchizedek was intended to prefigure the truly eternal, unending priestly ministry of the risen Christ. He officiates in the power of an endless life. The Mosaic Law which laid down Levitical succession lacked the ability to make anything perfect, including the Aaronic order of priesthood; the law was ultimately weak and unprofitable. The "hope", referring to the access to God of His New Testament people, is better in all respects and has a glorious perfection, or completeness, which the old covenant lacked.

It is the better nature of the *covenant* which is next stressed, based as it is on a divine oath. For in contrast to the priests of the house of Levi, He, the Lord Jesus Christ, has his priesthood rooted in the declaration of Psalm 110, "The Lord has sworn and will not repent, 'You are a priest forever according to the order of Melchizedek'". So, Jesus has become a surety, or guarantor, of a better covenant. Furthermore, verses 23 and 24 remind us that there were many (Levitical) priests, because they were prevented by death from continuing. But He, because He continues forever, has unchangeable priesthood."

So, to summarize the glory of Christ's office "according to the order of Melchizedek", we see that its legal basis is eternally secure in a divine oath. The oath established the eternal character of the office; the risen Victor over death is its guarantor, or surety; and, as a result, it is unchangeable, in every respect better than the old; in short, perfect! The very last verse of chapter 7, verse 28, says just this. "For the law appoints as high priests men who have weakness, but the word of the oath, which came after the law, appoints the Son who has been perfected forever".

The intervening verses, 25 to 27, contain, however, a precious commentary on the importance of these great facts for the daily life of God's people. The words begin with one of the "therefore's" of Hebrews: "Therefore he is able to save to the uttermost those who come to God through Him, since He ever lives to make intercession for them. For such a High Priest was fitting for us, who is holy, harmless, undefiled, separate from sinners, and has become higher than the heavens: who does not need daily, as those high priests, to offer up sacrifices, first for His own sins and then for the people's, for this He did once for all when He offered up Himself.

Salvation to the uttermost - back to the theme of perfection and completeness. This is about His ministry of intercession for his own, who come to Him for that daily aid, or comfort, we thought of previously, which it is His prerogative as a priest to supply.

The writer pauses here, and we with him, to glory in the complete sacrifice of sin made by the sinless Son of God. We have already quoted chapter 10 where this tremendous truth is further declared: "we have been sanctified through the offering of the body of Jesus Christ once and for all ... For by one offering He has perfected forever those who are being sanctified" (vv.10,14). As they read these words, the Jewish believers addressed in this epistle would have recalled the old priestly ritual summed up in the words, "first for their own sins, then for the people's". Now, for them and for us, it is a spotless Son perfected for evermore, and no endless repetition of bloodshed and burning; everything is fulfilled and made perfect in Christ.

And so, chapter 8 open with the words, "Now this is the main point of the things we are saying. We have such a High Priest, who is seated at the right hand of the throne of the Majesty in the heavens, a Minister of the sanctuary and of the true tabernacle which the Lord erected, and not man." The expression "such a High Priest" sums up all the wonders of Christ's Person and office that we have been thinking about; and then remind us of the heavenly *place* He occupies at the Father's right hand. It is the place where He ministers, or serves, that is now the sanctuary as far as God is concerned. The precious, if shadowy, teaching of the Tabernacle in the wilderness has come to fulfilment, and we remember that, in its day, it represented only a holy place made with hands, as chapter 9 verse 24 tells us. *We* have come to eternal reality. Truly, old things are passed away, and all things have become new in this priestly sphere of service.

Next is the statement that "every high priest is appointed to offer both gifts and sacrifices. Therefore it is necessary that this One also should have something to offer." Verse 4 of chapter 8 points out that Christ could have no part in any continuing service of the earlier sanctuary which still operated according to the law of Moses, and was associated with the copy and shadow; a copy and shadow be it noted, which was true to the pattern Moses had been given, but still no more than a copy and shadow. "But now he has obtained more excellent ministry", we read in verse 6, "inasmuch as He is also Mediator of a better covenant, which was established on better promises."

So our divine High Priest, the Lord Jesus Christ, in His more excellent ministry should also, we are reminded, have something to offer. This something is not elaborated here for we have more to consider yet about the basis of this service in a covenant. But let us note that later in this epistle, in chapter 13 verse 15, we do read about sacrifices that a holy priesthood offers to God through their great High Priest. Also in the first epistle of Peter we have instruction about this, at which we shall look further in a later chapter.

———————

In Christ the Lord our eyes behold

A thousand glories more

Than the rich gems and polished gold

The sons of Aaron wore.

They first their own sin-offering brought

To purge themselves from sin;

His life was pure, without a spot

And all his nature clean.

Fresh blood as constant as the day

Was on their altars spilt.

But His one offering takes away

For ever all our guilt.

Their priesthood passed through several hands

For mortal was their race;

His never-changing office stands

Eternal as His days.

Their range was earth, nor higher soared,

The heavens of heavens is His;

There, in His majesty, the Lord

A Priest forever is.

Eternal glories crown His name,

As Prophet, Priest and King;

Soon heaven and earth shall sound His fame,

Each day fresh praises bring.

CHAPTER NINE: COVENANTS OLD AND NEW

=====

We now take up our study of the epistle to the Hebrews at the seventh verse of chapter 8. This verse reads as follows: "For if that first covenant had been faultless, then no place would have been sought for a second." So we are returning for some further examination of the comparison of the old covenant with the new. We have been left in no doubt by earlier verses that the new covenant is a better one. It is associated with the better hope in chapter 7 that we have already commented on, and we shall see in Hebrews 9 that it is linked to better sacrifices. Altogether, this reminds us again that "better" is one of the key words in this epistle. We met it in the introduction when we considered how that the Lord Jesus is so much better than the angels, having inherited a more excellent name than they.

We shall encounter it further in later chapters concerning the riches of the inheritance belonging to the people of God. The use of the word "better" at repeated intervals, and in a variety of context in Hebrews, serves to reaffirm the character of the New Testament truths presented. Similarly, the writer's return here in chapter 8 to the theme of the covenant, ensures that we do not lose sight of the deep underlying truths and principles in the epistle. It is reminiscent of the work of a composer in creating a symphony. A theme is struck and, then repeatedly emerges. It is elaborated on and increased in melodic richness.

So now we have returned to theme of a new covenant and a fresh resonance is struck by reference to the ancient prophet Jeremiah. The old covenant was flawed, for Israel found themselves quite incapable of living up to it. So much so that their failure deteriorated into calamity evidenced by captivity of Israel first, then of Judah. Just when such a pall of darkness had fallen over His chosen people, God, in His encouraging grace, raised up Jeremiah and other prophets to offer a better prospect; to light a national beacon of hope which would sustain God-fearing men and women in days of humiliation and suffering.

Said Jeremiah, as quoted here, "Behold the days are coming", says the LORD, "when I will make a new covenant with the house of Israel and with the house of Judah – not according to the covenant that I made with their fathers ... because they did not continue in my covenant ... For this is the covenant that I will make with the house of Israel: After those days", says the LORD, "I will put My laws in their mind and write them on their hearts; and I will be their God, and they shall be My people."

And Jeremiah goes on to add the crowning reassurance, "For I will be merciful to their unrighteousness, and their sins and their lawless deeds I will remember no more". The final comment of the author of Hebrews is, "In that he says, 'A new covenant', He has made the first obsolete. Now what is becoming obsolete and growing old is ready to vanish away" (Heb.8:8-13).

The Hebrew disciples addressed here had already learned at their conversion about the importance of the blood of a new covenant; about the death of Christ as its secure basis. The focus now concerning the better new covenant is on its impact on the nation of Israel to which these Christians belonged, and to whose history the writer is now appealing.

We do well to keep reminding ourselves of pressure these people were constantly under to renounce their new faith and settle for the old spiritual economy offered to Israel in the Law of Moses. Here, by taking up the prophecy of Jeremiah, the Holy Spirit is making a broad sweep of Israel's past, present and future. For the assurances here to the nation of Israel carried their thought away forward to a day when God will again restore His people who were set aside for a season, as Paul declared with a heavy heart in his epistle to the Romans. There, Paul points forward to a day when "the fullness of the Gentiles has come in and so all Israel will be saved." Paul there quotes from Isaiah 59, "The Deliverer will come out of Zion, and He will turn away ungodliness from Jacob; for this is My covenant with them, when I take away their sins" (Rom.11:25-27). This is the same covenant, the new covenant that we are reading about in Hebrews, linked here, as there, to the glory of taking away sin.

Now most of the teaching in the epistle to the Hebrews concerns the spiritual service of the people of God today, of which these Jewish saints were part. They, with Gentile brothers and sister, were sharers in the holy priesthood service in the sanctuary under the gracious ministry of our heavenly High Priest, officiating according to the order of Melchizedek.

But at this point in the writing they were being reminded that the new covenant terms and promises were very much associated with the nation of Israel as such. Those gathered as the people of God today and serving in His house, comprise Jews and Gentiles, the Gentiles by far the majority.

But the glorious sweep of new covenant truth has also a special message for Israel. When the Lord returns and the unbelieving nation of Israel experiences what a hymn graphically describes in the words, 'deeply mourning shall their own Messiah see,' then in contribution and repentance, there will be a national turning to Christ and an entering into the riches of the new covenant, with sins and iniquities no more remembered. Adding this grand prospect to the present enjoyment of a new covenant truth as centered in Christ, only underlines still further the obsolete nature of the old covenant and all that it stood for. "Ready to vanish away" are the closing word of chapter 8.

But this did not mean that there was nothing left to be learned from the first covenant, its imagery was rich, and its foreshadowing of new covenant truths was most helpful in our understanding of these. So chapter 9 opens with, "... even the first covenant had ordinances of divine service and the earthly sanctuary". We shall see in due course how comparison and contrast are again employed in the following through the matter of access to God's presence in old and new covenants, and how all the details dealt with shed light on our understanding of the service of the holies today, and on the glorious person and work of Christ.

O Lord, Thy courts we humbly tread,

By Thy blest Spirit hither led,

We bring our sacrifice of praise

Adoring Thee in grateful lays.

Accepted through His death are we,

To be a priesthood, serving Thee,

What joy is ours through saving grace,

To worship in the Holy Place.

Thus boldly we now enter in,

Cleansed by Christ's blood from every sin;

It speaks for us before Thy throne,

Proclaims redemption's work is done.

Great God, Thy love all love excels;

It humbles us, yet praise compels!

Eternally our song shall be

Of Him who said, "Remember Me."

CHAPTER TEN: THE GOOD THING TO COME

———

We have seen in our study of Hebrews so far that the immense superiority of the new covenant over the old is a major theme. The writer seeks to impress on his Jewish Christian reader that they have inherited in Christ something far better than they had before. Therefore they should never consider reverting to the service of the Temple and the Law of Moses, as they were being pressed to do by fellow Jews. In chapter 9 of the epistle, which we have now reached, we have a demonstration of the value of the contents and furniture of the original tabernacle as an illustration of new spiritual realities.

The opening verses of chapter 9 offers a brief recap of the two tabernacle compartments and their furnishings: "For a tabernacle was prepared: the first part, in which was the lampstand, the table, and the shewbread, which is called the sanctuary; and behind the second veil, the part of the tabernacle which is called the Holiest of All, which had the golden altar of incense and the ark of the covenant overlaid on all sides with gold, in which were the golden pot that had the manna, Aaron's rod that budded, and the tablets of the covenant; and above it were the cherubim of glory overshadowing the mercy seat."

Then the words are added, "of these thing we cannot now speak in detail". The writer was eager to get on to speaking about the *service* of the tabernacle and how it foreshadowed the priestly service of the people of God today in the heavenly sanctuary. He knew that most, if not all of his reader would be familiar with the physical details of the Tabernacle and subsequent temple.

Perhaps one thing in Hebrews 9 verses 3 and 4 should be commented on. That is the association here of the golden altar of incense with the Holiest of All, or the Holy of Holies, the innermost room of the Tabernacle to which only the high priest had access on the annual Day of Atonement. Students of the Tabernacle will be well aware that this golden altar actually stood in the previous compartment, called the Holy Place. So why say here that the innermost place "had the golden altar of incense"? The explanation surely is that, although the golden altar stood in the Holy Place, it *belonged* to the Holy of Holies as is suggested in the first book of Kings chapter 6:22 where we read, "he overlaid with gold the entire altar that was by the inner sanctuary."

Another version refers to it as the altar "that belonged to the oracle". It related closely to the special service of the Holy of Holies; yet being physically in the Holy Place, it was possible for the priests there to burn the incense associated with the regular morning and evening sacrifices. This is what verse 6 of our chapter reminds us, "the priests always went into the first part of the tabernacle, performing the services."

Then we are reminded that only the High Priest entered the Holy of Holies and "not without blood, which he offered from himself and for the people's sins committed in ignorance". We have earlier been reminded of this and, in our symphony of truth, this theme will recur again and again. God had in mind a freer access to the Most Holy Place as the central glory of "the good things to come" of verse 11; access for all His people to His own immediate presence, but one which could not be offered in association with the earthly tabernacle. The gifts and sacrifices associated with that "cannot", we are told, "make him who performed the service perfect in regard to the conscience" (v.9).

We are coming now right to the heart of the matter concerning the ritual cleansing and the fundamental difference presented by the cleansing power of the blood of Christ. If the Hebrew saints could grasp this in all its glory, they would never want to look back to their old attachment to the Law and the Temple. The crucial difference was that cleansing under the old covenant was a symbolic purification of the flesh, while that offered by the death of Christ is a definitive purification of the conscience. We must quote in full the powerful words of verses 11 to 15 for they bring this out with clarity and assurance:

"But Christ came as High Priest of the good things to come, with the greater and more perfect tabernacle not made with hands that is, not of this creation. Not with the blood of goats and calves, but with His own blood He entered the Most Holy Place once for all, having obtained eternal redemption. For if the blood of bulls and goats and the ashes of a heifer, sprinkling the unclean, sanctifies for the purifying of the flesh, how much more shall the blood of Christ, who through the eternal spirit offered Himself without spot to God, purge your conscience from dead works to serve the living God? And for this reason He is Mediator of the new covenant, by means of death, for the redemption of the transgressions under the first covenant, that those who are called may receive the promise of the eternal inheritance."

To attempt a detailed exposition of those great words is beyond us now. They not only point up, as we have seen, the issue of the cleansing of the conscience by the death of Christ. They also assure these dear beleaguered Jewish converts to Christ that He, the Mediator of the new covenant, has by His death effected 'the redemption of the transgressions under the first covenant, that those who are called may receive the promise of the eternal inheritance'. The verse just quoted reminds us to that the Lord entered, with His own blood, the heavenly sanctuary 'having obtained eternal redemption'. All the accumulated sins of the centuries under the old covenant, which had only been covered by animal sacrifices in anticipation of Calvary, were now dealt with in full and final settlement.

The truths of inheritance and redemption were very important to the Jewish people. But until the coming of Christ, and His death and resurrection, their ideas about inheritance and redemption were confined mainly to this world. They did not have a clear vision of eternal redemption, or of eternal inheritance; here was something truly glorious. The blood of sacrificed animals as we have noted, brought a cleansing which was both temporary and, though also symbolic, physical in its immediate application – "cleansing of the flesh" are the words. Now, through the redemptive work of Christ, is offered a purging of conscience, once and for all accomplished, truly eternal in its effectiveness.

And let us not fail to note and appreciate the profound truth contained in verse 14 where we are instructed that, "Christ, through the eternal Spirit, offered himself without spot to God". In the process of bringing to all redeemed a true and eternal cleansing from sin, as indicated by the reference to conscience, we learn that the work of Calvary was an act of the Godhead. This is expressed in terms which defy full understanding, but command worship and awe. God the Son, offering himself as a spotless sin-offering to God the Father, through the eternal spirit. Perhaps that last expression is the most difficult for out finite minds to penetrate. But at all events it conveys the wonder of the triune God at Calvary working as One "for us men and for our salvation" as the Catechism so tellingly puts it.

The death of Christ is also linked in this passage of Hebrews to the need for a testator's death to take place before the testament or covenant he made can become effective; and we are reminded of the covenant significance of blood sprinkling. For Moses, when delivering the law from Sinai, took the blood of the sacrifices and, we read, "sprinkled both the book itself and all the people, saying, 'This is the blood of the covenant which God has commanded you." This was followed by the sprinkling of the Tabernacle and all its vessels. A summing-up word of profound importance follows: "And according to the law, almost all things are purged with blood, and without shedding of blood there is no remission."

As we read this, the lovely echo of the Lord's words in the Upper room returns, "This is my blood of the new covenant, which is shed for many for the remission of sins."

CHAPTER ELEVEN: PERFECTED FOR EVER

―――――

As we saw in the last chapter, chapter 9 of Hebrews strikes a note of fundamental truth - "without the shedding of blood there is no remission" (v.22). In century after century, this truth had been pressed home in the experience of Israel as they offered their prescribed sacrifices day by day, festival by festival and year by year on the annual Day of Atonement. The author of Hebrews is about to remind us yet again of the fuller truth about the heavenly place into which God's people today enter into worship, as they serve in His spiritual house.

First, this rock-like principle must be established in our minds – no shedding of blood, no remission of sins. But we will be reminded in verse 28 that, "Christ was offered once to bear the sin of many." We pause in wonder to thank God for that marvel of divine grace. Speaking of the sacrifices of the old covenant, we now read in verse 23 of chapter 9, "Therefore it was necessary that copies of the things in the heavens should be purified with these, but the heavenly things themselves with better sacrifice than these'. Here again is the contrast between the transient nature of Tabernacle and Temple service, and the eternal reality in heaven to which God's people today may come.

In the old, the sprinkled blood served its covenant significance. In the new, the blood of Christ is the means by which entry to the heavenly sanctuary is secured. We have already rad in verse 11 that, "Christ came as High Priest of the good things to come ... not with the blood of goats and calves, but with His own blood He entered the Most Holy Place once for all, having obtained eternal redemption."

Now verse 24 tells us that "Christ has not entered the holy places made with hands, which are copies of the true, but into heaven itself, now to appear in the presence of God for us". We may not readily understand why "the things in the heavens" need a cleansing process by the blood of Christ; perhaps the thought is sanctification of these things and places in heaven which now come into their own as a place of spiritual worship; no longer serving mainly as a pattern for something temporary on earth.

At all events He, our Redeemer and Priest, has gone in and it is not a question of repeated sacrifice, 'not that He should offer Himself often', as the text has it. The contrast is with the High Priest of Israel entering on the annual Day of Atonement. If that pattern were to continue "He then would have had to suffer often since the foundation of the world; but now, once at the end of the ages, he has appeared to put away to put away sin by the sacrifice of Himself".

The Lord Jesus Christ is described in the book of Revelation chapter 13 verse 18 as "the Lamb slain from the foundation of the world". That is how the redemptive work of Calvary is seen in the perspective of God's eternal purposes; yet the accomplishment of that purpose of grace was achieved "once at the end of the ages"; and the words in verse 28 of Hebrews chapter 9 correspond perfectly: "So Christ was offered once to bear the sins of many", and the words are added, "To those who eagerly wait for Him, he will appear a second time, apart from sin, for salvation" – the words which point so clearly and directly to the believer's full realization of salvation at the personal return of the Lord from heaven.

But we have so far omitted mention of verse 27, which immediately precedes the words about the Lord's return. "And as it is appointed for men to die once, but after this the judgment, so Christ was offered ..." and so on. Why this solemn word inserted at this point in a discussion of the wonderful finished work of Christ? It seems to be a reminder of Christ's identification with men and women in the matter of death and judgment. All men have an appointment with death, and judgment follows – an inevitable sequence in God's purpose for mankind. So the Son of Man, the last Adam has gone down into death once also and into judgement; God's judgement on human sin, 'to bear the sin of many' as the scripture here puts it. Therefore, although this verse is an integral part of the truth about the priestly work of Christ for God's people, it is also appropriate that the verse be taken and used to impress on unbelievers the solemnity of death and the following judgement. It is a verse which the Holy Spirit has used to arrest many a person about the one appointment all must keep.

The verses which follow at the beginning of Hebrews chapter 10 reassert the triumphant truth of the putting away of sins by the sacrifice of Jesus, and re-emphasize the shadowy, repetitive nature of the old covenant sacrifices. These were incapable of bringing the offerer into a completely satisfactory relationship with God. "For the law", says the text, "having a shadow of the good things to come, and not the very image of the things can never with these same sacrifices, which they offer continually year by year, make those who approach perfect". Otherwise they would have ceased, having removed the consciousness of sin. In fact they mainly serve as a reminder of sin.

We are taken now by the writer to Psalm 40 which provides one of these very clear prophetic messages about the coming One. "Sacrifices and offering You did not desire, but a body You have prepared for Me. In burnt offering and sacrifices for sin You had no pleasure. Then I said, 'Behold I have come – in the volume of the book it is written of Me - to do Your will, O God." Having first disposed of the old covenant sacrifices as providing God with no lasting pleasure or satisfaction, the Psalmist emerges into the sunny uplands of divine grace, "Behold, I have come to do Your will, O God." Then the definitive word, "He takes away the first that he may establish the second" (v.9).

Can our Jewish Christian friends, to whom this letter first came, now begin to grasp fully the marvelous truth being presented to them? As far as God is concerned, the old inferior things that they are being constrained by some to revert to, have been "taken away". They are gone; they belong to a past that God wants them to consider completely finished. That is God's will for them and for us, and the fulfillment of that divine work fell to our wonderful Saviour, Redeemer, and now High Priest.

Then we have the words, "By that will we have been sanctified through the offering of the body of Jesus Christ once for all". Please, dear Hebrew saints, burdened by the pressures on you, take this gem of divine truth and treasure it above all else. Realize that the same purpose which saw the Lamb of God slain from the foundation of the world, has embraced you. You have been sanctified. Look back to the Cross of Christ outside the holy city, and look back no further. Rely on "the offering of the body of Jesus Christ once for all". That is enough!

This precious truth is reiterated in verse 14 in the words, "For by one offering He has perfected forever those who are being sanctified", words which follow another reminder of the old covenant priests standing offering daily the same ineffectual sacrifices. Christ by contrast, having offered one sacrifice for sins forever, has sat down at the right hand of God, waiting for His enemies to be made His footstool.

The closing words of this section of the writing take us back again to Jeremiah 31, already quoted in chapter 8, about the new covenant promised to Israel, and close with the words "Their sins and their lawless deeds I will remember no more". The writer's final summing up is, "Now where there is remission of these, there is no longer an offering for sin". So this past chapter of God's dealing with men about sin, redemption and access to His presence in worship, is decisively closed. We can move on to what all this means for a redeemed, worshipping people today.

CHAPTER TWELVE: TO ENTER THE HOLY PLACE

Our study continues with verse 19 of Hebrews chapter 10. This contains one of the most significant 'therefore's' of this epistle. "Therefore, brethren, having boldness to enter the Holiest by the blood of Jesus, by a new and living way which He consecrated for us, through the veil, that is, His flesh, and having a High Priest over the house of God, let us draw near with a true heart in full assurance of faith, having our hearts sprinkled from an evil conscience and our bodies washed with pure water."

The Jewish disciples who received this letter have already in earlier verses been referred to by the writer as "brethren". This was most noticeable and deliberate in the second chapter where the term is first applied as coming from the Lord Himself when we read, "For both He who sanctifies and those who are being sanctified are all of one, for which reason He is not ashamed to call them brethren saying, "I will declare your name to My brethren' in the midst of the congregation I will sing praise to You"' (vv.11,12). The context there is the collective praise and worship of God's people. Now again in the important passage we are considering, we have the term "brethren" applied in the context of collective priestly service in the heavenly holy place.

The entry invited is "with boldness" - the boldness of confidence in the word and promise of God; in fulness of faith in the revelation of the new covenant and its effects, "Boldness to enter the holy place by the blood of Jesus". That was the means by which He entered, as we have seen – "with His own blood" - and it is the only means of access for His own today. That access is also described as "by a new and living way which He consecrated for us, through the veil, that is His flesh." It has already been plainly stated that our sanctification is through the offering of the body of Jesus Christ once for all. Here the purposes of the incarnation of the Son of God find a sure fulfillment in ushering a redeemed and sanctified people into the Father's presence.

So we may draw near, having a High Priest over the house of God, with a true heart, in full assurance of faith. Also, we rest in the truth of the sprinkling of the covenant blood which effects the cleansing of conscience. The expression, "our bodies washed with pure water" surely corresponds to "the washing of regeneration" of which Paul writes to Titus. This is the anti-type and spiritual fulfilment of the washing by Moses of Aaron and his sons at the laver of the Tabernacle in preparation for priestly service in God's house. For it is the house of God today in which Christ is said to be High Priest.

This very important, indeed unique reference in the New Testament to collective priestly worship in the very presence of God is couched in very few words. It is not the writer's purpose at this point to go into a lot of detail on this subject, although I am sure many students of the Word must have wished that he had taken it a little further! And it is true that we have some further important things to hear in the passage in chapter 13, verses 10 to 15, about the heavenly service to which God's people have been brought. It does, however, seem appropriate at this point to look at what we are instructed elsewhere in the New Testament scriptures about the collective priestly service prescribed for disciples today.

We find an important reference to this in 1 Peter chapter 2. There believers are spoken of as "living stones" coming to Him, the Lord Jesus, Himself a Living Stone: "You also", we read, "as living stones, are being built up as a spiritual house, a holy priesthood, to offer up spiritual sacrifices acceptable to God through Jesus Christ". Here we have a "spiritual house", surely the house referred to in our passage in Hebrews chapter 10, verse 21 as "the house of God". We have a "holy priesthood", to be identified with the "holy brethren" of Hebrews chapter 3, verse 1, who are partakers of the heavenly calling; and the "brethren" invited here in chapter 10 to enter the holy place with boldness.

Then, in 1 Peter chapter 2 we have the expression, "spiritual sacrifices", which can be related to chapter 13, verse 15, "the sacrifice of praise to God, that is the fruit of our lips, giving thanks to His name"; as well as taking our thoughts back to chapter 8 verse 3. There, you will remember, we read about our great High Priest, that it is necessary that He also should have something to offer. As the priests of Israel took the sacrifice made on behalf of God's people and presented it to God, so today our High Priest takes the offerings, or spiritual sacrifices, of His people to offer to His Father. Let us note carefully that all of this is in the context of God's house, for the living stones of 1 Peter chapter 2 have to be built up to be a spiritual house.

The analogy of the building of Solomon's Temple is striking. Stones were prepared at the quarry. But a careful building process had to take place exactly according to the plan and pattern given for the house. So today disciples of Christ, living stones, do well to examine the New Testament for the pattern of God's house. It is a question many might ask, "Can this beautiful presentation in Hebrews of collective priestly service by a sanctified people of God today, really be seen in diffuse and diverse groupings of believers with widely differing forms of worship?" For surely it was of importance to God under the old covenant that His people were closely integrated as such, so that only one form of priestly service was offered which followed His own word and command. So, in 1 Peter chapter 2, the spiritual house, the holy priesthood of today, is called a chosen generation, a royal as well as holy priesthood, a holy nation and a special people.

Coming now to Hebrews chapter 10 verse 23, we have the words, "Let us hold fast the confession of our hope without wavering, for He who promised is faithful". This recalls to our minds the words of chapter 3 verse 6 where we read of God's house, "whose house we are if we hold fast the confidence and the of the hope firm to the end." We note then that this indicates a conditional character for God's house, leading us to conclude that not all who have eternal life through faith in Christ necessarily have a part in the house of God and its service - another stimulus to challenge our hearts about a place in God's house today. We are also to "consider one another in order to stir up love and good works", and, "not forsaking the assembling of ourselves together, as is the manner of some, but exhorting one another, and so much more as you see the Day approaching".

It is clearly of great importance to the Lord that the sanctity and preciousness of holy priesthood service by His people should be matched by Christ-like conduct, and regular gathering for worship and service. This too is in sympathy with the apostle Peter's teaching which we have been considering. The same people who form a holy priesthood in worship and the offering up of spiritual sacrifices, are a royal priesthood who "proclaim the praises (or show forth the excellencies) of Him who called you out of darkness into His marvellous light, who once were not a people but are now the people of God, who had not obtained mercy but now have obtained mercy" (1 Pet.2:9).

Into Thy holy presence,

O God, we venture now,

With reverent hearts and holy awe

Before Thy throne to bow.

We plead not our own virtues,

They cannot here avail.

But by the blood of Jesus,

We enter through the veil.

No guilty fears assail us,

As those defiled with sin,

But as a holy priesthood now

With joy we enter in.

Our great High Priest before us

Has opened up the way,

And clothed in His perfection

We would our homage pay.

Through Him our sacrifices

Acceptable will be,

Though not of earthly gifts received,

We tender unto Thee.

To sacrifice of praises

That unto Thee ascends,

His blessed name and person

An incense fragrance lends.

For the gift Thou gavest,

Thy Son from heaven above,

We thank Thee, Lord

We praise Thee, Lord

Thou God of matchless love.

CHAPTER THIRTEEN: A FEARFUL THING

─────

In the previous chapter, we noted that in Hebrews chapter 10, there is something of a climax reached in the teaching about the Lord's high priesthood, and the priestly service of God's people today. The words, "Therefore, brethren, having boldness to enter the Holiest by the Blood of Jesus", draw together all the previous teaching, and assure the people of God that they are invited as priestly worshippers into the very presence of God "by the blood of Jesus, by a new and living way which He consecrated for us, through the veil, that is His flesh". We saw that the word "boldness" is used and later, "full assurance of faith", all confirming to us the purpose of God in a special people, "a people for God's own possession" as the words of 1 Peter 2:9 appear in the Revised Version.

We went on to link this passage in the first epistle of Peter with our text here in Hebrews chapter 10 and saw that Peter unmistakably brings together the truths about living stones built up a spiritual house, about a holy and royal priesthood, and about a holy nation and a people of God. Reference back to Hebrews chapter 3 reminds us that Christ, as well as being High Priest is described "as a son, over God's house; whose house are we, if we hold fast our boldness and the glorying of our hope firm unto the end".

We have recapitulated a little because we need to keep the conditional nature of God's house and its service before our minds when we come to the later verses of Hebrews chapter 10. We need to appreciate that the very solemn words which follow are addressed to disciples of Christ who had been admitted to all the precious and holy privileges of priestly service in God's house. They had turned their backs on Jewish ritual and the inferior content of the old covenant requirements; they had embraced the glory of divine grace in Christ, and entered the privileges of New Covenant truth. The epistle in their hands had, up to now, been full of strong encouragement from them to continue in this, and not be seduced back to lesser things.

Now in chapter 10 verse 26 they have to be warned that it would be no light thing at all if this tragedy happened. Here are the opening words of this, one of the severest warning passages in this or any other New Testament epistle. "For if we sin willfully after we have received the knowledge of the truth, there no longer remains a sacrifice for sins, but a certain fearful expectation of judgment and fiery indignation which will devour the adversaries". The writer goes on then to refer back to the application of Mosaic law to the person who deliberately turned his back on God's commandments, and continues, "of how much worse punishment, do you suppose, will he be thought worthy who has trampled the Son of God underfoot, counted the blood of the covenant by which he was sanctified a common thing, and insulted the Spirit of grace?"

This is strong stuff! This is not a gentle warning about the day-by-day failures the Christian is aware of in his or her life; not even those in which there may be an element of wilful choice, as there so often is. This is a situation of deliberate apostasy; of going over to the enemy in full understanding of what it means, for it is about persons who have "received the knowledge of the truth". Such people know and understand clearly the faith they have embraced and all the precious truth that is associated with it; truth beautifully and carefully expounded in the chapters of Hebrews we have been studying. And now they are quite deliberately repudiating this so as to bring the gospel of Christ into common contempt and, effectively, to insult the Holy Spirit.

We are warned in Scripture about grieving and quenching the Holy Spirit in our Christian lives because of spiritual failure. But this is a wilful and deliberate standoff, hurling insults at the divine Spirit from the ranks of the enemy. This was the awful position into which the saints receiving this letter could be drawn if they yielded to the pressure of their persecutors. And if that happened they would come under the severe judgment of God as God's people. Deuteronomy chapter 3 is cited, "Vengeance is Mine; I will repay" and, "the LORD will judge His people". No wonder the chilling words follow, "It is a fearful thing to fall into the hands of the living God".

Many an earnest Christian, on reading this passage, has asked himself, "Could I ever reach such a fearful position; and if so, what is the nature of the judgment here pronounced?" First of all let us say without hesitation that the surest sign that a child of God is far from such a condition is his or her fear of it. Hebrews chapter 10 speaks of those who show arrogant defiance and frank rebellion against God and the revelation of truth He has granted them. Let us keep fresh in our hearts a healthy dread of such a thing overtaking us, and an unfaltering desire to remain loyal to the One who revealed His free grace and truth to our hearts. But the nature of the judgment referred to - what is this? Can a true believer be lost eternally? Is this implied in the language used here?

––––––––––––––

IN ANSWERING THIS WE must return to a principle often stated, namely the understanding of one passage of scripture alongside others which deal with the same theme. As we saw when considering chapter 6, it is not possible to go into detail about the teaching of the New Testament on the eternal security of the child of God. Inherent in such truths as the new birth, as taught to Nicodemus in John chapter 3, and the sealing of the Holy Spirit as clearly set out in Ephesians chapter 1, there is a principle of permanence and eternal certainty about the salvation which comes with faith in Christ. Speaking of His sheep, Jesus said, "I give them eternal life, and they shall never perish".

Those referred to so severely in Hebrews 10 verse 26 "have received the knowledge of the truth" and so are clearly united to Christ by eternal bonds. But it is still a fearful thing to fall into the hands of the living God, and this must refer to the rejection and destruction of the life of a person who wilfully repudiates his faith. Let us recall again Paul's first letter to the Corinthians chapter 3, "If anyone's work which he has built ...

endures, he will receive a reward. If anyone's work is burned he will suffer loss; but he himself will be saved, yet as by fire". Not only will the judgment seat of Christ be a fearful time for the apostate Christian, but even in this life he may know much judgment and suffering; suffering of many kinds under the hand of God, including that of a guilty conscience if denied repentance for a time by the Lord; for it is He and He alone who grants repentance.

But, thank God, the author of Hebrews had more comforting or words to add for those receiving this stringent warning. He recalls their early days of Christian testimony, the great struggle with sufferings which they had endured; their fellowship in suffering with others who were persecuted; and their kindness to the brother now writing to them. "In my chains" is how he puts it, doubtless referring to dark days of imprisonment.

They had joyfully accepted the plundering of their goods, "knowing that you have a better and an enduring possession for yourselves in heaven". Do not cast away your confidence, they are encouraged, "you have need of endurance, so that after you have done the will of God, you may receive the promise". What promise? Here it is: "For yet a little while, and He who is coming will come and will not tarry. Now the just shall live by faith, but if anyone draws back, My soul has no pleasure in him".

———————

WITH SUCH A PRECIOUS prospect of the Lord's return, they could gladly receive the final encouragement, "But we are not of those who draw hack to perdition, but of those who believe to the saving of the soul". Perdition would be the total failure of their life work. Perish such a thought! By the grace of God they, and we, can know by faith the salvation, or preservation, of our lives for His glory.

CHAPTER FOURTEEN: BY FAITH WE UNDERSTAND

———

We now consider Hebrews chapter 11, probably one of the best known and most quoted passages of the New Testament. "Now faith is the substance of things hoped for, the evidence of things not seen." These words open what has often been described as a word picture gallery of men and women of faith. And so it is, as the verses unfold revealing the exploits of truly great people of the Old Testament; touching on their motives and demonstrating the outcome of their lives which was so glorifying to God.

It is important to notice how this marvelous passage links on to the closing verse of chapter 10 of the epistle. The thought there is of the deep solemnity of the warning given against repudiation of the faith these Jewish Christians had embraced. This was followed, however, by a strong encouragement which finished with the words, "But we are not of those who draw back to perdition, but of those who believe (or 'have faith' as the Revised Version has it) to the saving of the soul". What better to reinforce that faith than a review of the conquering experiences of past men and women of their own chosen race who, in their day, had faced persecution, hardship, contempt and martyrdom in the resolute exercise of their faith; whose life and witness had shown the glory and triumph that could shine through suffering and form vital links in the chain of testimony which led to those reading this letter. The last verse of chapter 11 will bring this out clearly. Of course, the Holy Spirit had very much in mind the stream of encouragement and inspiration that this chronicle of lives would send away down the centuries right to our own day.

So, "the assurance" or "the substance" of things hoped for is the definition given of faith in the opening words. It is "the proving" of things not seen. These words spell out a deep sense of conviction that the revelation of God about matters vital to all human beings, life, death, and eternity, is true and reliable. It is a settled confidence in the reality of things that are invisible to physical perception, but of which God speaks in language and actions which command respect and acceptance.

Reading the opening verses of Hebrews 11 brings to mind the experience of Thomas. How that dear disciple must have longed all the rest of his life that the Lord had never needed to say to him, "Thomas, because you have seen Me you have believed. Blessed are those who have not seen and yet have believed" (John 20:29). Not that any of the other disciples would claim to have excelled Thomas in faith; perhaps they had not had quite the same demands made on their faith.

Verse 2 of our great chapter on faith states that, "... by it (that is, faith) the elders obtained a good testimony". J.B. Phillips explains this point well in his translation: "It was this kind of faith that won their reputation for the saints of old". Then before launching into his list of illustrious examples of men and women of faith beginning with Abel, the writer makes a majestic declaration on the application of faith to the truths of creation. "By faith we understand that the words were framed by the word of God, so that the things which are seen were not made of things which are visible".

This is an affirmation of confidence in the Genesis record from Moses about the Lord of the universe at work in creation. It proclaims trust in the divine inspiration of David's words in Psalm 33. "By the word of the LORD the heavens were made, and all the host of them by the breath of His mouth. He gathers the water of the sea together as a heap; He lays up the deep in storehouses. Let all the earth fear the LORD; let all the inhabitants of the world stand in awe of Him. For he spoke, and it was done; He commanded, and it stood fast".

Later, the words of John chapter 1 were to be written. "In the beginning was the Word and the Word was with God and the Word was God". Also, such language as Colossians chapter 1 verses 15-17 which demonstrate in resounding terms the divine creatorship vested in the person of the Lord Jesus Christ; "the Word"; "the firstborn of all creation" in whom "all things consist (or hold together)".

It is worth at this point pausing for a moment on the word used here and translated "worlds" in the expression "we understand that the worlds were formed by the word of God". It is a Greek word which can equally be translated "the ages". Again, Mr. Philips seemed to get it just about right when he translated this as, "the whole scheme of time and space". Alford, the great authority on New Testament Greek said, "The expression 'the ages' includes in it all that exists under the conditions of time and space themselves, conditions which do not bind God, and did not exist independently of Him, but are themselves the work of His Word'.

Some readers will be much more able than most to relate such words to the profound theories of time, space and matter developed in the minds of geniuses like Einstein and Hawking. But we can all surely glimpse the relevance of such words of Holy Scripture to the amazing concepts developed by modern mathematics and astronomy. Minds not trained or competent in these disciplines (and that means most of us) can only marvel and worship.

And the difference between the person of faith and an unbeliever is exposed in devastating fashion in Paul's letter to the Romans. He writes, "For since the creation of the world His invisible attributes are clearly seen, being understood by the things that are made, even His eternal power and Godhead, so that they are without excuse (Rom.1:20).

CHAPTER FIFTEEN: NOT ASHAMED TO BE CALLED THEIR GOD

———

It will be helpful and encouraging to look now at some of the distinguished characters named in Hebrews chapter 11, men and women of outstanding faith whose lives glorified God in their day, and who provide a shining example for us today. For although their circumstances were very different from ours, human nature does not change fundamentally and, even more important, our God's faithfulness is invariable. So our dear fellow disciples who received this letter originally, must learn that their new Master is the same yesterday, today and forever, words we find in the closing chapter of this letter.

Abel is the first name mentioned in the honours list of faith, and this is probably because his faith is notably linked to the important matter of sacrifice. Not that his parents, Adam and Eve, did not learn the need for animal sacrifice, but Abel's experience highlighted the vital element in sacrifice - the shedding of blood. His brother Cain had missed that point, or more likely knew of it but considered that he could devise a better way of pleasing God. So Cain became typical of men and women down the centuries – 'I'll do it my way'. But Abel "offered to God a more excellent sacrifice", one which reflected the significance of Calvary and foreshadowed the truth already expounded in chapter 10 of Hebrews. "For by one offering He has perfected forever those who are being sanctified". So Abel, we read, "obtained witness that he was righteous". And what is more, through his sacrifice, "he, being dead, still speaks". Noble witness was Abel though his life was so cruelly cut short.

Next in the train of witnesses is Enoch. In his case the witness was not so much to the principle of sacrifice, though doubtless Enoch was devout and diligent in that matter too. "By faith Enoch", we read, "was translated so that he did not see death ... for before his translation he had this testimony, that he pleased God". Godliness was the key to Enoch's life. What a contrast was the end of his earthly life with the violent tragic death of Abel! Yet both men pleased God and their witness honored Him. Jim Elliot died a violent death in the Ecuadorean Jungle, taking the gospel to the Aucas, while David Livingstone passed quietly away in his jungle hut as he walked through Africa with God. Such are the different outcomes of God-honouring lives within His all-wise purposes.

A pause in our text now while a vital principle is underscored, "without faith it is impossible to please Him, for he who comes to God must believe that He is, and that He is a rewarder of those who diligently seek Him". No principle is more fundamental to the Christian life; no other calls for more diligent and prayerful attention. "By faith Noah" are the next words we come to in verse 7, and the principle of this man's life, we are told, was godly fear. Moved by this, and being divinely warned, he prepared an ark for the saving of his household, by which he condemned the world and became heir of the righteousness which is according to faith. We cannot stay to reflect on the magnitude of faith which must have been needed to fulfil the charge that God gave Noah concerning the ark and the coming flood. The fear of God, which we are reminded in Proverbs is the beginning of wisdom, controlled Noah and fuelled his remarkably constant faith over all the testing years of the ark's building.

Next among the cardinal virtues associated with faith, and sustaining its blessings, is obedience. "By faith Abraham obeyed". Is not this very often the acid test of faith? One of our best loved Christian hymns declares: "Trust and obey, for there's no other way, to be happy in Jesus, but to trust and obey." Sound words, which derive directly from the life experience of Abraham. He obeyed to go out, "not knowing where he was going". Not only did he go out by faith, but by the same virtue and power he "sojourned in the land of promise ... dwelling in tents with Isaac and Jacob" and "he waited for the city which has foundations, whose builder and maker is God".

Sarah is beautifully linked with Abraham in their steadfast trust in God over all the drawn-out years of waiting for Isaac. Sarah's faith, we learn, was the source of her strength to conceive seed and bear a child when she was past the age. From this faithful union was "born as many as the stars in the sky for multitude - innumerable as the sand which is by the sea shore".

So we learn that faith deals with the God of the impossible. Chapter 11 verses 13-16 sets out the vision of these men and women. They died in faith not having received (or realized) the promises. They saw them and they embraced them, confessing that they were strangers and pilgrims. "They desire a better, that is, a heavenly country". And because of this a faithful God has prepared for them a city.

We could stay long to reflect on these truths, so relevant to ourselves today, but the Spirit has more to say, staying initially with Abraham. We are taken to Mount Moriah where, by faith, Abraham "offered up his only begotten son". This was not an act of blind obedience, for Abraham, correctly, accounted that God was able to raise Isaac up, even from the dead. Our faith is tested by the well-documented truth of the resurrection of Jesus Christ. How much greater was Abraham's test - and response - of faith with no previous record of divine intervention in resurrection. We salute such a confidence, and revel in all the beautiful foreshadowings of Christ in the trial of Abraham at Mount Moriah.

Then, it was also by faith that Isaac blessed Jacob and Esau, and Jacob, in turn, blessed each of the sons of Joseph. The Genesis record of the patriarchs sparkles with gems of spiritual insight, all the result of faith, and the vision granted in return. Similarly, Joseph, we read, "when he was dying, made mention of the departure of the children of Israel, and gave instructions concerning his bones". The departure of the children of Israel out of Egypt was an event of the utmost historical importance in God's purposes, and could not have been anticipated at the moment of Joseph's death apart from the revelation granted to faith.

The next seven verses of Hebrews chapter 11 are devoted to the experience of Moses and the Exodus. Indirectly, and although they are not mentioned in the text by name, Moses' parents received the first accolade in this connection. "By faith Moses, when he was born, was hidden three months by his parents". The first reason given is touchingly human. "They saw that he was a beautiful child"; the second spelled out the quality of their faith, "they were not afraid of the king's command". A noble and resolute couple were Jochebed and Amram! And their example of faith was not lost on their family, including Moses. Verse 24 leaps over the years of Moses' childhood and palace education and brings us to one of the most glorious examples of faith in the whole of Scripture. "By faith Moses, when he came of age, refused to be called the son of Pharaoh's daughter, choosing rather to suffer affliction with the people of God than to enjoy the passing pleasures of sin, esteeming the reproach of Christ greater riches than the treasures of Egypt; for he looked to the reward."

How sharp is the focus of the vision given here to faith – "the reproach of Christ". Such an example is surely reflected in a once proud Pharisee from Tarsus. "But what things were gain to me, these I have counted loss for Christ. But indeed I also count all things loss for the excellence of the knowledge of Christ Jesus my Lord" (Phil.3:7,8).

CHAPTER SIXTEEN: LET US RUN WITH ENDURANCE

———

We continue with the record of faith in Hebrews chapter 11: "By faith Moses, when he came of age, refused to be called the son of Pharoah's daughter, choosing rather to suffer affliction with the people of God than to enjoy the passing pleasures of sin, esteeming the reproach of Christ greater riches than the treasures of Egypt; for he looked to the reward."

We hesitate to comment much on such a fulsome commendation of sacrificial faith; and we have earlier commented on the remarkable expression, "the reproach of Christ". We remember the Lord's words concerning Abraham that "he saw My day". Similarly, Moses must have had a perception by faith of the coming Christ and of His exemplary endurance of suffering, a rare glimpse of the clarity of spiritual vision which can be awarded to faith.

So by faith Moses, we read, chose to suffer; forsook Egypt (for he endured as seeing Him who is invisible); kept the passover and the sprinkling of blood; and passed through the Red Sea as by dry land. An outstanding catalogue of achievements, and all by faith. The Hebrew saints, as they read this, would have recalled the earlier reference in their letter to Moses as "faithful in all His (God's) house as a servant, for a testimony of those things which would be spoken afterwards" (Heb.3:5). So the

complete cycle of Moses' life and service was placed on record
and all sprang from his faith. The readers would doubtless
perceive the connection between Moses and the Christ who
was to come: who had come as far as they were concerned and
now claimed their allegiance.

The final example of faith in Hebrews 11 concerns the
conquest of Jericho and the faith of Rahab. By implication,
Joshua's faith is recorded as we read that, 'by faith the walls of
Jericho fell down'. And it was also by faith that Rahab did not
perish when she received the spies with peace.

The writer seems to check himself at this point, recalling that
volumes could be filled with the exploits of all the men and
women of faith who might reasonably receive a mention.
Almost despairingly he cries, 'And what more shall I say?' There
are Gideon, Barak, Samson, Jephthah, David, Samuel and the
prophets - and a host of others, he might have added: "who
through faith subdued kingdoms, worked righteousness,
obtained promises, stopped the mouths of lions, quenched the
violence of fire, escaped the edge of the sword, out of weakness
were made strong, became valiant in battle, turned to flight the
armies of aliens. Women received their dead raised to life again.
And others were tortured, not accepting deliverance, that they
might obtain a better resurrection. Still others had trials of
mocking and scourgings, yes, and of chains and imprisonment.
They were stoned, they were sawn in two, were tempted, and
were slain with the sword. They wandered about in sheepskins
and goatskins, being destitute, afflicted, tormented - of whom
the world was not worthy" (vv.33–38).

These words just called out to be quoted in full! They flow on in a glorious stream of noble resolve and patient suffering such as most of us will never come near to experiencing. Yet those to whom these words were originally written lived in days of fierce persecution, as have many Christians down the ages to the present day. They were not far away historically from the fearful years of the persecutions of Nero and his corrupt court. The sufferings of Old Testament saints set out here in all their gruesome yet glorious detail were to reappear in all their horror in a very short time. It may well be that some of those reading this epistle became victims themselves.

Yet even so, they had realized something Abraham, Moses, Samuel and all those honoured in this roll-call had missed. For "all these" we read, "having obtained a good testimony through faith, did not receive the promise, God having provided something better for us that they should not be made perfect apart from us." The fact that all those illustrious saints of the past had not realized in fulfillment the supreme promise of God concerning His Son, only enhances the marvel of their faith, and of the testimony that sprang from it. The point is now made that the fuller divine revelation given to New Testament saints is a wonderful completion of God's purpose begun in the lives of those heroes of the past. That purpose of grace begins to come together in a glorious unity of fulfillment. Hands are reached out over past centuries to link with those now expressing their testimony in their own times. We recall the opening words of chapter 1:

"God, who at various times and in different ways spoke in times past to the fathers by the prophets, has in these last days spoken to us by His Son, whom He has appointed heir of all things, through whom also he made the worlds; who being the brightness of His glory and the express image of His person, and upholding all the things by the word of His power, when He had by Himself purged our sins, sat down at the right hand of the Majesty on high."

Indeed these very last words of chapter 1 verse 3 are echoed in chapter 12 verse 2 to which we now turn for its connecting word with chapter 11: "Therefore, since we also, are surrounded by so great a cloud of witnesses, let us lay aside every weight, and the sin which so easily ensnares us, and let us run with endurance the race that is set before us, looking unto Jesus, the author and finisher of our faith, who for the joy that was set before Him endured the cross, despising the shame, and has sat down at the right hand of the throne of God."

The expression "so great a cloud of witnesses", surely referring to the shining company of the faithful in chapter 11, draws the disciples very near in spirit to their illustrious predecessors of the old covenant. Undergirded by the moral and spiritual support of such strong characters, they and we must resolutely "lay aside every weight, and the sin which so easily ensnares us". Using the analogy of the athlete who discard his encumbrances just as far as possible, so the disciple of Christ prepares himself for the contest of Christian life and testimony. The besetting sin referred to here has tended to be seen as some sin or temptation particularly relevant to an individual's experience.

This may be a valid interpretation, but in view of all that is presented to us in chapter 11, surely the ever-present temptation to unbelief is prominent in the writer's mind.

The source of the Christian's strength for the conflict and the race is in the Person of our glorious "author and finisher" of the faith. This is Jesus, no other. The Old Testament men and women of faith had, as we have seen, a vision before them which nerved their endeavor and resolution. So had our noble Author and Finisher – "the joy that was set before Him". What joy, we may ask? The prophet Isaiah, in his prophecy of the suffering of the Christ, wrote, "He shall see the travail of His soul and be satisfied". And all "because He poured out His soul unto death, and he was numbered with the transgressors." The sheer nobility of the work of Calvary is revealed in the strong words about His endurance of the Cross, namely, "despising the shame". This is turning the tables on that most hurtful of all human experiences, contempt. This is contempt for contempt. Marvelous Saviour – at the right hand of the throne of God!

CHAPTER SEVENTEEN: EARTHLY DISCIPLINE – HEAVENLY VISION

───

In recent chapters we have explored very briefly the wonders of Hebrews chapter 11 about the Old Testament heroes of faith, and followed through the "therefore" of chapter 12, verse 1, where the exhortation is to lay aside all spiritual hindrances in running the race set before us. Only by "looking unto Jesus", is this possible; only the Author and Perfecter of our faith can inspire us to exploits of faith, surrounded as we are by "so great a cloud of witnesses", an exemplary company of high spiritual achievers.

The Hebrews epistle now moves towards its closing messages for the beleaguered disciples who were addressed. Their mentor writes, as we have seen, been carefully balancing strong encouragement with solemn warning. Now in chapter 12 verse 3 we stay with the matter of the endurance of our Lord Jesus Christ, the endurance of the Cross with all its shame and loss. "For consider Him who endured such hostility from sinners against Himself, lest you become weary and discouraged in your souls. You have not yet resisted to bloodshed, striving against sin." There is something almost ominous in the words "not yet" when we consider how near in time these people were to the major persecutions and tribulations about to descend from their Roman masters. They were encouraged to recognize in suffering the reality of divine chastisement.

Perhaps if we had written to the disciples in all the circumstances they faced, we would have avoided too much reference to chastisement. After all they were laboring under numerous threats and above all needed encouragement and support. Both of these they received in this letter, but yet they are presented with some very robust treatment; they are not spared the necessity of spiritual rebuke and instruction about the response expected from mature Christians. Indeed, they are being shown the respect due to mature believers, even though in earlier verses they were reminded that some of them still needed milk and not solid food.

Well, here is some solid food now! You have forgotten they are told, some of the exhortations expressed in a composite quotation from Proverbs, Job and the Psalms: "My son, do not despise the chastening of the LORD, nor be discouraged when you are rebuked by Him; for whom the LORD loves He chastens, and scourges every son whom he receives. If you endure chastening, God deals with you as with sons."

Now this very form of address "sons" carries its own overtones of acknowledged maturity, with all the responsibilities which follow. Indeed, the very legitimacy of a person's sonship comes into question if no chastening at all is in evidence. Having respected our human fathers, "shall we", they are challenged, "not much more readily be in subjection to the Father of spirits and live?" Human rebukes and corrections from parents can only be "as seemed best for them", yet often based on very flawed judgment. The objective of divine corrections is "that we may be partakers of His holiness".

Now here is a lofty aspiration indeed and one which softens any blow with the assurance of love and grace. True, no chastening seems to be joyful for the present, but grievous. Nevertheless, afterwards it yields the peaceable fruit of righteousness to those who have been trained by it. Yes, beloved Jewish Christians, you are in training! Take full advantage of it for it is leading you to God.

So to another "therefore". "Therefore, strengthen the hands which hang down, and the feeble knees, and make straight paths for your feet". Having attended to mutual support and encouragement, there then comes the exhortation to "pursue peace with all men, and holiness, without which no one will see the Lord". These words align themselves perfectly with the Lord's own, "Blessed are the pure in heart for they shall see God". How quickly impurity clouds our vision of the glory of the Lord and the beauties of Christ.

Warning follows about falling short of the grace of God; falling short, that is, of the blessed and holy effect the grace of God should have on our lives. Examples are given of the defilements strewn across our path; any troublesome root of bitterness by which, be it noted, many become defiled, not only the person against whom the bitter feelings are directed: or it may be sexually immoral conduct or a profane fleshly attitude such as Esau showed. His sense of spiritual values was lost, and for some morsel of food he sold his birthright. What is more, his later remorse and regret were unproductive, for we read that he was rejected when he wanted to inherit the blessing, and found no place of repentance though he sought it diligently with tears. Whether it was just the blessing, or the repentance that he sought tearfully, it is certain that he received neither. Let us beware, it is God who grants repentance and, solemnly, may withhold it if our heart is not right in its humility before him.

From verse 18 to verse 24 of Hebrews chapter 12 we have a unique passage of New Testament scripture. It is time for the writer to emphasize again to his readers the glory and majesty of the things associated with their New Testament heritage; and to do this in dramatic fashion by comparing the material things of the ancient service of Israel with a glimpse of the heavenly things which the people of God today have "come to". In the words of verse 18, God's collective people today, those we have earlier seen are built up a spiritual house to be a holy and royal priesthood, may come to the throne of grace for help and mercy, as seen in chapter 4; and they may approach into the heavenly sanctuary as worshippers, as in chapter 10. The heavenly place to which they come is here more fully described and contrasted with the earthly things Israel knew in the past.

Two verses are devoted to a reminder of the awesomeness of Mount Sinai at the giving of the Law – the fire, darkness, tempest, trumpet sound. Even Moses is quoted in the words, "I am exceedingly afraid and trembling". "You have come", the Hebrew disciples were told, "to Mount Zion and to the city of the living God, the heavenly Jerusalem, to an innumerable company of angels, to the general assembly and the church of the firstborn who are registered in heaven, to God the Judge of all, to the spirits of just men made perfect, to Jesus the Mediator of the new covenant, and to the blood of sprinkling that speaks better things than that of Abel". We cannot attempt an exposition of all these "wonderful things", to borrow the words of Howard Carter the archaeologist when he first gazed into the tomb of Tutankhamun, "I see wonderful things!" Wonderful indeed!

What, for example, is the relationship, if any, between this "heavenly Jerusalem" and other New Testament expressions such as "the Jerusalem above which is our mother" in Galatians; or the "new Jerusalem" described in Revelation? It will be fascinating one day to discover; similarly with expressions such as "general assembly and church of the firstborn." Enough to know that they are heavenly institutions and groupings ordained by God which adorn that glorious place. Above all its other glories is "Jesus the Mediator of the new covenant". There, too, is His precious sprinkled blood speaking of "better things than that of Abel". Quite a vision of celestial wonders to inspire the hearts and ambitions of the saints; and quite a challenge to our appreciation of new covenant blessings.

The closing words of chapter 12 are somber and arresting. "See that you do not refuse Him who speaks." These things are not to be treated lightly; they proclaim the character of a holy God who speaks from Heaven. "For if they did not escape who refused him who spoke on earth, much more shall we not escape if we turn away from Him who speaks from heaven, whose voice then shook the earth." We remember the words of chapter 2, "how shall we escape if we neglect so great a salvation". Yes, God shook Mount Sinai, and He will in the future shake heaven and earth.

But there are things that cannot be shaken and which remain. "Therefore since we are receiving a kingdom which cannot be shaken, let us have grace, by which we may serve God acceptably with reverence and godly fear. For our God is a consuming fire." We may come short of many of the expectations of God's kingdom and of the custodianship entrusted to us as the "little flock" (Lk.12:31,32). But in itself that kingdom cannot be shaken; its character is invulnerable and lasting. Our part is to show true reverence and godliness in the face of the uncompromising purity of God.

CHAPTER EIGHTEEN: COMPLETE ... TO DO HIS WILL

———

We come now to the concluding chapter of this remarkable letter to the Hebrews in chapter 13. First some final exhortations which, if regarded diligently, would produce a rounded witness to the grace of God in the lives of saints. The paramount requirement is mentioned first, "Let brotherly love continue". It echoes the Lord's own words, "By this shall all men know that you are My disciples, if you love one another". Add hospitality to strangers, for by so doing some have entertained angels unwittingly. Also, remember prisoners and those who are mistreated. Some of these words just could not be more up-to-date. "Prisoners and those mistreated" offer a vivid description of a contemporary world full of refugees and political prisoners.

"Marriage is honorable among all, and the bed undefiled; but fornicators and adulterers God will judge. Let your conduct be without covetousness, and be content with such things as you have. For He Himself has said, 'I will never leave you nor forsake you'. So we may boldly say: 'The LORD is my helper; I will not fear. What can man do to me?'" (vv. 4-6).

The New Testament writers repeatedly show great sensitivity to the requirement of sexual purity; and again they reflect a concern about an evil which seems increasingly unrestrained in our own day, as indeed is greed and covetousness. We remember that when David was guilty of adultery with Bathsheba the wife of Uriah, it was covetousness, greed, which the prophet Nathan pin-pointed in his subtle parable. It constituted the *root* sin of David's adultery: untruthfulness, and murder, themselves the evil *fruits*.

Having offered some final moral directives, the writer of Hebrews proceeds to his closing spiritual instruction. "Remember those who rule over you, who have spoken the word of God to you, whose faith follow, considering the outcome of their conduct". This reminds us that there are those among the people of God who have a responsibility to rule in God's house. We pause here for a moment to reiterate a point made earlier. There is no human rule envisaged in connection with the Church the Body of Christ in which every child of God has a place. But in God's house where subject disciples are gathered for collective service and worship, there is such a thing. And in what might be called "a worst case scenario", those who rule may have to guide a church of God in its judgement of an erring saint, even calling for his or her excommunication. This surely happened in Corinth when Paul instructed, "put away from yourselves that wicked person".

The judgmental role of elders or overseers is not one that it is highlighted in Hebrews, but as we see, we are reminded of their office and exhorted to remember them (including in our prayers); to obey them (v.17); and to greet them (v.24). They need prayer, respect and fellowship in their very important work. And a great example for them in their conduct is offered to them, and to us, in verse 8: "Jesus Christ is the same yesterday, today and forever". How often a pure gem of truth appears in Scripture in the context of some very practical teaching. Here is one, like Father, like Son; for James in his epistle chapter 1 verse 17 says of the Father of lights, "with whom there is no variation of shadow of turning". We praise God for the perfect constancy and invariable character of our great God and Saviour Jesus Christ. Herein is provided a shining example for elders; and a steadying word about false teaching, as we see next.

For the next careful warning offered is, "Do not be carried about with various and strange doctrines." Some of these "strange doctrines", which even then were being peddled, involved food fads which were alleged, falsely, to contain some intrinsic spiritual value. "For it is good that the heart be established by grace, not with foods which have not profited those who have been occupied with them." Does this not ring a loud bell today in relation to cults and modern heresies?

Then verse 10, "We have an altar from which those who serve the tabernacle have no right to eat." Back we come for a final time to the contrast of the vanishing service of an old covenant people, and that of believers today gathered together as the people of God. Those who hold to the old pattern simply do not belong with this altar which speaks of Christ. There is a reminder here about the sacrifices in the past where the blood shed was brought into the sanctuary of the Tabernacle, and the bodies of the animals were burned outside the camp of Israel. These were sin offerings and very solemn in God's sight. They brought a very special foreshadowing of Christ as a final once-for-all sin offering.

"Therefore Jesus that He might sanctify the people with His own blood, suffered outside the gate. Therefore let us go forth to Him outside the camp, bearing his reproach" (vv.12, 13). The people of God today will find themselves outside with Him; outside of, and separate from, patterns of service and worship which do not conform to the biblical pattern of God's house and kingdom. In the days when Hebrews was written, the primary separation was from the old Judaism in which they had been brought up. Today it is more likely to be from movements and organizations, even of Christians, which have chosen paths that diverge from the New Testament teachings.

Separation *to*, and service *for*, belong together; so we have the words, "Therefore by Him let us continually offer the sacrifice of praise to God, that is, the fruit of our lips, giving thanks to His name". The writer of our letter is gathering up points now which he wishes, in conclusion, to leave in the minds of his readers.

"But do not forget to do good and to share, for with such sacrifice God is well pleased. Obey those who rule over you, and be submissive, for they watch out for your souls, as those who must give account. Let them do so with joy and not with grief, for that would be unprofitable for you."

So we have already commented on rules and their work. Finally, "pray for us; for we are confident that we have a good conscience, in all things desiring to live honorably. But I especially urge you to do this, that I may be restored to you the sooner". A very personal touch this by the writer who clearly had a great affection for the saints and longed to be with them.

The closing benediction of this epistle is very precious: "Now may the God of peace, who brought up our Lord Jesus from the dead, that great Shepherd of the sheep, through the blood of everlasting covenant, make you complete in every good work to do His will, working in you what is well pleasing in His sight, through Jesus Christ, to whom be glory for ever and ever, Amen."

Such benedictions almost defy too much comment. Their intrinsic eloquence and expressiveness are rich. The great Shepherd of the sheep, the blood of the new, eternal covenant which He shed, and triumphant resurrection he accomplished are the foundation of the completeness; a rounded spiritual wholeness of character, individual and collective, which will be truly well pleasing in His sight. Had the writer, I wonder, a final slight anxiety that all the strong words he had written in utter faithfulness might prove too strong meat for some? "And I appeal to you, brethren, bear with the word of exhortation, for I have written to you in a few words." Few words indeed! Something of an understatement, we might feel, but often as we have read we have felt that there was much more he wanted to say.

Now an intimate mention of their friend Timothy, and their joint desire to visit them. Then the final signing off ... "greet all those who rule over you, and all the saints. Those from Italy greet you, grace be with you all, Amen". Whether Paul wrote this epistle or not, this is a Pauline style of final greeting and we leave our brief study of an invaluable New Testament document with prayer that the Lord will bless our study of it together to His glory.

Did you love *Better! The New Covenant in Hebrews*? Then you should read *Blood Most Precious - A Bible Study* by EDWIN NEELY!

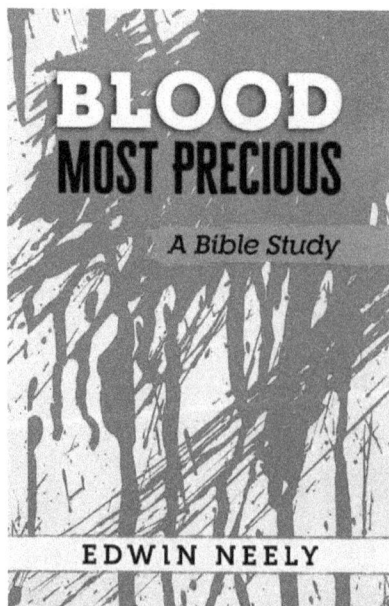

With no less than 375 Bible verses on the subject of blood, God definitely has something important to tell us about it. In this informative book, Edwin Neely explains its role and meaning under both the Old and New Covenants and its significance to us as Christians today – not just in our salvation, but in our service as well.

CHAPTER ONE: NON-SACRIFICIAL BLOOD

CHAPTER TWO: BLOOD IN NON-ALTAR SACRIFICES

CHAPTER THREE: THE SANCTITY OF THE BLOOD

CHAPTER FOUR: SPRINKLED BLOOD

CHAPTER FIVE: THE BLOOD OF THE SIN OFFERINGS

CHAPTER SIX: THE BLOOD OF THE SWEET SAVOUR OFFERINGS

CHAPTER SEVEN: AN ALTAR DRENCHED WITH BLOOD

CHAPTER EIGHT: EFFECTS OF BLOOD FOR THE BELIEVER TODAY

CHAPTER NINE: THE CUP OF THE NEW COVENANT 'IN MY BLOOD'

CHAPTER TEN: THE THREE CROSSES

CHAPTER ELEVEN: OUR GREAT HIGH PRIEST

CHAPTER TWELVE: HALLELUJAH FOR THE BLOOD!

Also by JOHN TERRELL

John Terrell Box Set
Walking With God: Principles of Separation in Christian Life
and Service
The Search for the Truth of God
The Kingdom of God and the Holy Nation
Better! The New Covenant in Hebrews

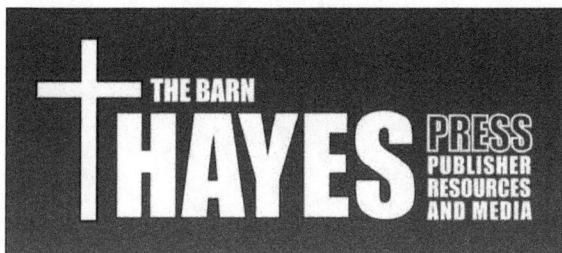

About the Publisher

Hayes Press (www.hayespress.org) is a registered charity in the United Kingdom, whose primary mission is to disseminate the Word of God, mainly through literature. It is one of the largest distributors of gospel tracts and leaflets in the United Kingdom, with over 100 titles and hundreds of thousands despatched annually. In addition to paperbacks and eBooks, Hayes Press also publishes Plus Eagles Wings, a fun and educational Bible magazine for children, and Golden Bells, a popular daily Bible reading calendar in wall or desk formats. Also available are over 100 Bibles in many different versions, shapes and sizes, Bible text posters and much more!